WEB TECHNOLOGIES: THEORY & PRACTICALS

AUTHOR

Dr. Raman Dugyala

Professor, Computer Science Engineering
Chaitanya Bharathi Institute of Technology, Gandipet
Hyderabad, Telangana - 500075

REVIEWER

Dr. Rahul Johari

Associate Professor, Guru Gobind Singh Indraprastha University,
University School of Information and Communication Technology,
E-Block, Sector 16c, Dwarka, Delhi - 110078

KHANNA BOOK PUBLISHING CO. (P) Ltd.
4C/4344, Ansari Road, Darya Ganj,
New Delhi, India

All India Council for Technical Education
Nelson Mandela Marg, Vasant Kunj,
New Delhi, India

Dear Readers,

To prevent the piracy, this book is secured with HIGH SECURITY HOLOGRAM on the front title cover. In case you don't find the hologram on the front cover title, please write us to at contact@khannabooks.com or whatsapp us at +91-99109 09320 and avail special gift voucher for yourself.

Specimen of Hologram on front Cover title:

Moreover, there is a SPECIAL DISCOUNT COUPON for you with EVERY HOLOGRAM.

How to avail this SPECIAL DISCOUNT:

Step 1: Scratch the hologram

Step 2: Under the scratch area, your "coupon code" is available

Step 3: Logon to www.khannabooks.com

Step 4: Use your "coupon code" in the shopping cart and get your copy at a special discount

Step 5: Enjoy your reading!

ISBN: 978-93-5538-305-1

Book Code: DIP471EN

Web Technologies: Theory and Practicals

by Dr. Raman Dugyala

First Edition: 2026

Originally Published by:

All India Council for Technical Education, Ministry of Education, GOI

Exclusively Published & Distributed by:

Khanna Book Publishing Co. (P) Ltd.
4C/4344, Ansari Road, Daryaganj,
New Delhi (INDIA)

Visit us at: **www.khannabooks.com**
Write us at: **contact@khannabooks.com**

To view complete list of books, Please scan the QR Code: KPH

Printed in Bharat.

प्रो. टी. जी. सीताराम
अध्यक्ष
Prof. T. G. Sitharam
Chairman

सत्यमेव जयते

आज़ादी का अमृत महोत्सव

अखिल भारतीय तकनीकी शिक्षा परिषद्
(भारत सरकार का एक सांविधिक निकाय)
(शिक्षा मंत्रालय, भारत सरकार)
नेल्सन मंडेला मार्ग, वसंत कुंज, नई दिल्ली–110070
दूरभाष : 011–26131498
ई–मेल : chairman@aicte-india.org

ALL INDIA COUNCIL FOR TECHNICAL EDUCATION
(A STATUTORY BODY OF THE GOVT. OF INDIA)
(Ministry of Education, Govt. of India)
Nelson Mandela Marg, Vasant Kunj, New Delhi-110070
Phone : 011-26131498
E-mail : chairman@aicte-india.org

FOREWORD

Engineers are the backbone of any modern society. They are the ones responsible for the marvels as well as the improved quality of life across the world. Engineers have driven humanity towards greater heights in a more evolved and unprecedented manner.

The All India Council for Technical Education (AICTE), have spared no efforts towards the strengthening of the technical education in the country. AICTE is always committed towards promoting quality Technical Education to make India a modern developed nation emphasizing on the overall welfare of mankind.

An array of initiatives has been taken by AICTE in last decade which have been accelerated now by the National Education Policy (NEP) 2020. The implementation of NEP under the visionary leadership of Hon'ble Prime Minister of India envisages the provision for education in regional languages to all, thereby ensuring that every graduate becomes competent enough and is in a position to contribute towards the national growth and development through innovation & entrepreneurship.

One of the spheres where AICTE had been relentlessly working since past couple of years is providing high quality original technical contents at Under Graduate & Diploma level prepared and translated by eminent educators in various Indian languages to its aspirants. For students pursuing 2nd year of their Engineering education, AICTE has identified 87 books, which shall be translated into 12 Indian languages - Hindi, Tamil, Gujarati, Odia, Bengali, Kannada, Urdu, Punjabi, Telugu, Marathi, Assamese & Malayalam. In addition to the English medium, books in different Indian Languages are going to support the students to understand the concepts in their respective mother tongue.

On behalf of AICTE, I express sincere gratitude to all distinguished authors, reviewers and translators from the renowned institutions of high repute for their admirable contribution in a record span of time.

AICTE is confident that these outcomes based original contents shall help aspirants to master the subject with comprehension and greater ease.

T.G. Sitharam

(Prof. T. G. Sitharam)

ACKNOWLEDGEMENT

I am grateful to many individuals and organizations who have supported me throughout the process of writing this book.

First and foremost, I would like to thank **Rahul Johari**, the reviewer of this book, who provided valuable feedback and suggestions that helped me improve the content and presentation. His expertise and insights have been immensely helpful in shaping this book into its final form.

I would also like to express my sincere appreciation to the All India Council for Technical Education (AICTE) for their support and encouragement in undertaking this project. Their commitment to fostering excellence in technical education has been a constant source of inspiration.

I am also indebted to the various contributors, books, publications, and articles in the field of web technologies that have informed and enriched this book. Their scholarship and research have been instrumental in advancing the field and have served as a valuable resource for this work.

Finally, I would like to acknowledge the publishing house for their professionalism, expertise, and guidance throughout the publishing process. Their commitment to quality and excellence has been evident at every stage, and I am grateful for their support in bringing this book to fruition.

Thank you all for your invaluable contributions and support. This book would not have been possible without you.

Dr. Raman Dugyala,

Professor, Computer Science Engineering.

PREFACE

The book titled "Web Technologies" is a result of my extensive experience in the field of web development and design. The aim of this book is to introduce the graduate level students to the world of web technologies, and provide them with a comprehensive understanding of the subject matter.

The explosive technological advancements in web development have made it an integral part of our daily lives. Therefore, it is important for students to have a strong foundation in this field. This book is written according to the syllabus provided by AICTE, and covers all the essential topics in a simple and easy-to-understand language.

During the writing process, I have referred to various standard textbooks, publications, and articles in the field, in order to ensure that the content is up-to-date and relevant. In addition, I have also included QR codes in all the units, which students can scan to access additional information and resources related to specific topics.

The book covers the basics of web development, along with the latest advancements in the field. The content is presented in a logical and systematic manner, and numerous examples and illustrations have been included to aid in understanding the concepts better. The book also includes a set of practice exercises and problems, which will help students to apply the concepts they have learned.

I hope that this book will serve as a valuable resource for students, and will inspire them to pursue a career in web development. I would like to express my gratitude to the reviewers who have provided their valuable feedback and suggestions to make this book better. I would also like to acknowledge the contributions of various publications, books, and articles that have helped me in writing this book. Finally, I would like to thank the publishing house for their support and assistance in bringing this book to fruition.

Dr. Raman Dugyala,
Professor, Computer Science Engineering.

OUTCOME BASED EDUCATION

For the implementation of an outcome based education the first requirement is to develop an outcome based curriculum and incorporate an outcome based assessment in the education system. By going through outcome based assessments, evaluators will be able to evaluate whether the students have achieved the outlined standard, specific and measurable outcomes. With the proper incorporation of outcome based education there will be a definite commitment to achieve a minimum standard for all learners without giving up at any level. At the end of the programme running with the aid of outcome based education, a student will be able to arrive at the following outcomes:

Programme Outcomes (POs) are statements that describe what students are expected to know and be able to do upon graduating from the program. These relate to the skills, knowledge, analytical ability attitude and behaviour that students acquire through the program. The POs essentially indicate what the students can do from subject-wise knowledge acquired by them during the program. As such, POs define the professional profile of an engineering diploma graduate.

National Board of Accreditation (NBA) has defined the following seven POs for an Engineering diploma graduate:

PO1. Basic and Discipline specific knowledge: Apply knowledge of basic mathematics, science and engineering fundamentals and engineering specialization to solve the engineering problems.

PO2. Problem analysis: Identify and analyses well-defined engineering problems using codified standard methods.

PO3. Design/ development of solutions: Design solutions for well-defined technical problems and assist with the design of systems components or processes to meet specified needs.

PO4. Engineering Tools, Experimentation and Testing: Apply modern engineering tools and appropriate technique to conduct standard tests and measurements.

PO5. Engineering practices for society, sustainability and environment: Apply appropriate technology in context of society, sustainability, environment and ethical practices.

PO6. Project Management: Use engineering management principles individually, as a team member or a leader to manage projects and effectively communicate about well-defined engineering activities.

PO7. Life-long learning: Ability to analyse individual needs and engage in updating in the context of technological changes.

COURSE OUTCOMES

By the end of the course the students are expected to learn:

CO-1: The necessary background in matrices and determinants so as to apply them in finding solutions and aid in interpreting/analysing linear systems, optimization tactics.

CO-2: Determining the area and volume especially by applying simple techniques of Integral calculus.

CO-3: To analyse that coordinate geometry provides a connection between algebra and geometry through graphs of lines and curves.

CO-4: To tell the difference between a resultant and a concurrent force; to interpret and analyse simple physical problems in the form of a differential equation.

CO-5: To explore and visualize data by using the applicability of topics learnt and also with the help of some basics of MATLAB.

Mapping of Course Outcomes with Programme Outcomes to be done according to the matrix given below:

Course Outcomes	Expected Mapping with Programme Outcomes (1- Weak Correlation; 2- Medium correlation; 3- Strong Correlation)						
	PO-1	**PO-2**	**PO-3**	**PO-4**	**PO-5**	**PO-6**	**PO-7**
CO-1	3	3	3	3	1	1	3
CO-2	3	2	2	2	1	1	3
CO-3	3	2	2	2	1	1	3
CO-4	3	2	2	3	1	1	3
CO-5	3	3	3	3	1	1	3

GUIDELINES FOR TEACHERS

To implement Outcome Based Education (OBE) knowledge level and skill set of the students should be enhanced. Teachers should take a major responsibility for the proper implementation of OBE. Some of the responsibilities (not limited to) for the teachers in OBE system may be as follows:

- Within reasonable constraint, they should manoeuvre time to the best advantage of all students.
- They should assess the students only upon certain defined criterion without considering any other potential ineligibility to discriminate them.
- They should try to grow the learning abilities of the students to a certain level before they leave the institute.
- They should try to ensure that all the students are equipped with the quality knowledge as well as competence after they finish their education.
- They should always encourage the students to develop their ultimate performance capabilities.
- They should facilitate and encourage group work and team work to consolidate newer approach.
- They should follow Blooms taxonomy in every part of the assessment.

Bloom's Taxonomy

Level	Teacher should Check	Student should be able to	Possible Mode of Assessment
Create	Students ability to create	Design or Create	Mini project
Evaluate	Students ability to justify	Argue or Defend	Assignment
Analyse	Students ability to distinguish	Differentiate or Distinguish	Project/Lab Methodology
Apply	Students ability to use information	Operate or Demonstrate	Technical Presentation/ Demonstration
Understand	Students ability to explain the ideas	Explain or Classify	Presentation/Seminar
Remember	Students ability to recall (or remember)	Define or Recall	Quiz

GUIDELINES FOR STUDENTS

Students should take equal responsibility for implementing the OBE. Some of the responsibilities (not limited to) for the students in OBE system are as follows:

- Students should be well aware of each UO before the start of a unit in each and every course.
- Students should be well aware of each CO before the start of the course.
- Students should be well aware of each PO before the start of the programme.
- Students should think critically and reasonably with proper reflection and action.
- Learning of the students should be connected and integrated with practical and real life consequences.
- Students should be well aware of their competency at every level of OBE.

CONTENTS

1 Introduction to WWW

UNIT SPECIFICS

Through this unit we will discuss the following aspects:

- *Protocols and Web Programs related to Web Browser;*
- *Web Browser and Server and It's Configuration;*
- *Users Logging to the server;*
- *Dynamic IP and Web Designing Principles ;*
- *Planning the site and Navigation;*

RATIONALE

This unit focuses on the World Wide Web as a platform for social services, content publication, and interactive applications. Understanding the underlying technology, the formats and standards on which the web is built, as well as the evolution of the World Wide Web and related technologies, is necessary for developing web-based applications. - The World Wide Web's client-server architecture, its communication protocols, and the concepts of web design. - Languages and formats used in contemporary web pages

PRE-REQUISITES

Problem Solving Skills

Object Oriented Programming

UNIT OUTCOMES

List of outcomes of this unit is as follows:

U1-O1: Describe basic Protocols related to web Browsers

U1-O2: Describe the Design of Web Application

U1-O3: Explain the configuration of the web server and it's architecture.

U1-O4: Explain the Designing principles of Website.

U1-O5: Apply planning and designing principles to construct a website

Unit-1 Outcomes	EXPECTED MAPPING WITH COURSE OUTCOMES (1- Weak Correlation; 2- Medium correlation; 3- Strong Correlation)				
	CO-1	CO-2	CO-3	CO-4	CO-5
U1-O1	3	3	3	-	-
U1-O2	2	2	2	-	-
U1-O3	3	3	3	2	-
U1-O4	2	2	3	1	-
U1-O5	3	3	3	2	-

1. PROTOCOL:

A protocol is basically a standard that makes it possible to connect, communicate, and transfer data between two locations on a network. In other words, the protocols are digital languages that are implemented as networking algorithms. Users use several networks and network protocols when surfing.

1.1. Types of protocols:

I. HTTP:

The Hyper Text Transfer Protocol (HTTP) is a standard for information transfer on the internet that is used to transfer hypertext documents. The formatting and transmission standards are described in this protocol. It also details the various actions web browsers are expected to take in response to requests to access a particular web page. Every moment a person launches a web browser, they are inadvertently using HTTP, which is the protocol used to share text, images, and other multimedia on the World Wide Web.

II. HTTPS:

Hypertext Transfer Protocol over Secure Socket Layer is known as HTTPS. Consider it an HTTP version with security. Most websites that request personal or sensitive information do so via HTTPS (such as a password or your credit card details).

SSL is used when you view a website utilising HTTPS (Secure Sockets Layer). An SSL certificate must be deployed on the server for a website to use HTTPS. These are typically issued by a Certificate Authority, which is a reputable third party (CA).

When utilising HTTPS to browse a website, you can view the SSL certificate's details. You may, for instance, verify its legitimacy. You might also make sure the website really does belong to the company you believe it does. Typically, you can do this by twice clicking on the padlock icon on the browser. You only see the padlock icon when you access a secure website.

III. FTP

Its shorthand name is FTP, or File Transfer Protocol. Online file transfers are done with it. Updates to a website are routinely uploaded through FTP by web developers (i.e., to upload a new version of the website).

In contrast to HTTP, which uses it to display the file in your browser, FTP just uses the file to send it from one computer to a specific location on another computer. FTP can be used to transfer files from your computer to a remote computer, such as a web server, or from the distant computer to your local computer.

IV. TCP/IP

Different computer types can communicate with one another using the Transmission Control Protocol/Internet Protocol. The IP protocol requires that each computer connected to the Internet have a special serial number, or IP address. TCP specifies how data should be converted into IP packets and how it should be transferred across the internet. It also verifies that the message was transmitted to the intended recipient correctly and that the packets contain information about the message's source, destination, and the sequence in which the message contents should be reassembled.

V. SMTP

These protocols, such as the Simple Mail Transfer Protocol, are necessary for sending and dispersing outbound emails. This protocol adds the message to the list of outgoing mails after reading the recipient's email address from the message header. Additionally, it removes the email from the outgoing list after sending it to the recipient's email address.

VI. TELNET

Terminal Network: The TCP/IP protocol TELNET is used by the ISO's virtual terminal service. This makes it possible for local machines to connect to one another. The computer that is connected is referred to as the remote computer, and the computer that is connecting is referred to as the local computer. We can view any activity taking place on the remote computer in the local computer using TELNET operation. This uses the client/server model to operate. The telnet client programme is used by the local computer, while the telnet server application is used by the remote computer.

VII. POP3

Post Office Protocol 3: POP3 is the abbreviation for Post Office Protocol version 3. Both of its message access agents (MAAs), the client MAA and the server MAA, are utilised to access the messages in the mailbox. We can retrieve and manage emails from the mailbox on the recipient mail server to the recipient's computer with the aid of this protocol. Between the receiver and recipient mail server, this is implied.

1.2. WEB PROGRAM

Web program is a code for a web page. You need a web browser to run a web page source code. Just like any program you require different languages to code a webpage. HTML is the most basic language used to create a webpage.While there are many different programming languages, the most common ones used in web development are JavaScript, HTML, CSS, PHP etc.,

1.3. SECURE CONNECTION

To protect the data being transferred from one machine to another, secure connections must be able to do three things.

i. Stop unapproved individuals from acquiring critical information

ii. It must first verify the person requesting access to and sharing data is who they say they are.

iii. It must prevent information from being seen or altered by anonymous individuals.

Although there are numerous ways to create a secure connection, most of them include data encryption. Data encryption is a technique for keeping information secret from unauthorised third parties. On both computers connected using this method, an appropriate programme that can encrypt and decode data must typically be installed. These are the fundamental security protocols that are part of popular communication protocols including TCP/IP, HTTPS, POP3 and IMAP. In rare cases, firewalls and antivirus programmes can also help establish secure connections.

1.4. WEB APPLICATION

A Web application (Web app) is an application software that is supplied over the Internet by way of a browser interface and is kept on a remote server. By definition, web services are web applications, and many websites—though not all—contain web applications.

Anybody, from a business to a person, can use web applications for a variety of reasons and for a wide range of objectives.

Some examples of regularly used Web apps are online calculators, webmail, and e-commerce sites. While certain Web apps can only be viewed by a particular browser, the majority of Web apps are available regardless of the browser.

1.4.1 How Web applications work

Downloading is not required for web apps because they may be accessed via a network. Users can access a Web application with a web browser like Google Chrome, Mozilla Firefox, or Safari.

A web app can't run without a database, an application server, and a web server. Web servers manage client requests while the application server completes the assigned work. A database can be used to store anything that has to be kept.

Web apps can be developed by small development teams and frequently go through short development cycles. JavaScript, HTML5, or Cascading Style Sheets (CSS) are used to develop the bulk of web apps.

These languages are frequently employed for client-side programming, which helps develop an application's user interface.

A Web application's scripts are created using server-side programming. Languages like Python, Java, and Ruby are often used in server-side development.

1.4.2 Advantages:

There are numerous uses for web applications, and these usage offer numerous potential advantages. Common advantages of Web applications include:

- Providing access to the same application version for numerous users.
- Web apps don't require installation.
- You can see web apps on a range of gadgets, such as a desktop, laptop, or smartphone.
- Accessible with a variety of browsers.

1.5. Web Developments tools

Building websites and apps for the internet, or an intranet, is a process known as web development. Writers of the code that defines things like style, layout, and interactivity are known as web developers. They work to make a website's design and functionality come to life. All of the tools we use online, from the most basic static web pages to social media platforms and applications; e-commerce websites to content management systems (like WordPress), have been created by web developers..

The frontend, the backend, and database technology are the three different sorts (or layers) of web development. Frontend development, also referred to as client-side scripting, includes all of the components of a website that the user sees and interacts with directly. The frontend is responsible for things like menus, contact forms, and layout.

The focus of backend development, often known as server-side scripting, is on the background operations. The frontend notifies the backend when you interact with a website in some way, such filling out a form and clicking "submit." In response, the backend sends the necessary data to the frontend, such as the code required to display a message like "Thank you for completing this form."

Technology related to databases makes up the third layer. All files and content required for a website to run are stored in the database in a manner that makes it simple to access, organise, update, and save.

A fully functional website or application is created and maintained by combining the efforts of the frontend, backend, and database technologies. As a result, these three layers serve as the basis for web development.

Web developers can test and debug their code using web development tools, often known as devtools or inspect elements. They differ from website builders and integrated development environments (IDEs) in that they serve as tools for assessing a website's or web application's user interface rather than being directly involved in the creation of a webpage.

Web browsers either have built-in functions or add-ons that are used for web development. Most popular web browsers, such as Google Chrome, Firefox, Internet Explorer, Safari, Microsoft Edge and Opera, have built-in tools to help web developers, and many additional add-ons can be found in their respective plugin download centres.

Developers can work with a range of web technologies thanks to web development tools. including HTML, CSS, the DOM, JavaScript, and other components that are handled by the web browser. Due to increasing demand from web browsers to do more, popular web browsers have included more features geared for developers.

1.6. WEB BROWSER

A web browser, sometimes known as a browser, is a piece of software used to access content on the World Wide Web. Chrome, Firefox, Safari, Internet Explorer, Microsoft Edge, Opera, and UC Browser are the most widely used browsers.

1.7. Web Server

A web server is a device that uses the internet to deliver content or services to users. A physical server, server operating system, and software that supports HTTP communication make up a web server.

A web server is a piece of software that responds to requests issued by users' computers through HTTP by using HTTP to provide files that produce web pages to those users.

- A web server is also known as an internet server.
- Web servers are essential to any type of web hosting.
- A lot of web hosting companies decide which web servers to use depending on the demands of their customers, the number of customers they can fit on a single server, the programmes and software they use, and the amount of traffic each customer generates. Therefore, choose a web server that adheres to the requirements.

A web server can be any server that transmits an XML document to another device. A more accurate description of a web server would be one that delivers content and services in response to HTTP requests.

A web server is always linked to the internet. A unique address will be assigned to each web server that connects to the Internet.

In order to meet the needs of its customers, hosting providers use various web servers.

I. Apache web server

One of the most widely used web servers created by the Apache Software Foundation.

- Apache is free and open-source software that works with practically any operating system, including Linux, UNIX, Windows, FreeBSD, Mac OS X, and others.
- Due to its modular design, the Apache web server is simple to customise. The fact that it is open source also implies that you can customise it to meet your needs by adding your own modules as needed.
- Compared to other web servers, it is more stable and makes handling administrative problems simpler. It is successfully installable across various systems.
- Handles multiple requests simultaneously using multithreading.

II. IIS web server

IIS is a Microsoft product (Internet Information Services).

- Because Microsoft developed and maintains this software, it is compatible with all Windows platforms..

- • However, it is not an open source project, therefore adding customised modules and making changes can be challenging.

III. Nginx web server

Nginx is another open-source, free web server. High performance, stability, ease of configuration, and resource efficiency are some of its best qualities.

- Instead of using threads to process requests, this web server employs an event-driven design that is far more scalable and requires minimal, predictable amounts of memory while it is under demand.

IV. LightSpeed web server

A high-performance drop-in replacement for Apache is LiteSpeed (LSWS). The most widely used commercial web server on the internet is called LSWS.

Switching to LiteSpeed for your web server will enhance performance and reduce running costs

1.8. DYNAMIC IP

When a computing device or network node connects to a network, it is given a temporary IP address called a dynamic Internet Protocol address (dynamic IP address). Every new network node is given a dynamic IP address, which is an automatically configured IP address, by a DHCP server.

Internet service providers and networks with a lot of connecting clients or end-nodes typically use dynamic IP addresses. Unlike static IP addresses, dynamic IP addresses are not permanent. A dynamic IP is assigned to a node until it's connected to the network; therefore, the same node may have a different IP address every time it reconnects with the network.

A Dynamic Host Configuration Protocol (DHCP) server controls the assignment, reassignment, and adjustment of dynamic IP addresses. One of the primary reasons behind having dynamic IP addresses is the shortage of static IP address on IPv4. Dynamic IP addresses allow a single IP address to be shuffled between many different nodes to circumvent this problem.

1.9. WEB DESIGNING

1.9.1 Principles of good Website design

An excellent website should engage visitors and effectively convey its desired message. Consistency, colours, font, graphics, simplicity, and usefulness are just a few factors that contribute to good website design.

Numerous significant design factors affect how a website is perceived. Creating trust with consumers is one way that a well-designed website can motivate people to take action. Making sure your website design is optimised for usability (form and aesthetics) and how easy it is to use is crucial to establishing a positive user experience (functionality).

I. Website purpose

The user's needs must be met by your website. Each page should have a straightforward goal to let the consumer interact with what you have to offer. What does your website aim to achieve? Are you delivering useful knowledge, such as a "How to guide"? Is it a website that offers amusement, such as sports coverage, or are you trying to sell the user something? Websites may serve a variety of functions, yet they all have certain fundamental goals;

- Defining Expertise
- Developing Your Reputation
- Creating Leads
- Sales and After Care

II. Simplicity

When thinking about how to improve your website's usability and user experience, simplicity is the best approach. Here are some strategies for designing for simplicity.

- **Colour**: Color has the power to evoke feelings and transmit messages. By selecting a colour scheme that complements your brand, you may influence how your customers interact with it. No more than five different colours should be used. Harmonious colour combinations are quite powerful. Appealing colour selections raise consumer engagement and enhance user mood.
- **Type**: On your website, typography has a crucial part to play. It grabs the audience's interest and serves as the visual representation of the brand voice. On the website, typefaces should be readable, and there should be no more than three different fonts.
- **Imagery**: An image is any visual device used in communication. This includes not only still photography, but also film, illustration, and all forms of graphics. Every image used by the corporation should reflect its brand identity while also capturing the spirit of the enterprise. It's important to utilise high-quality images as a first impression to give visitors a sense of professionalism and credibility because the majority of the initial information we ingest on websites is visual.

III. Navigation

Users interact with the navigation system on websites to find the content they are looking for. A website needs good navigation to keep users there. If a website's navigation is challenging, visitors will give up on using it and search elsewhere for what they need. It's critical to maintain consistent, simple-to-use navigation throughout each page.

IV. F-shaped pattern reading

The most popular pattern used by website visitors to scan text is the F-based pattern. According to eye-tracking studies, people tend to focus mostly on the top and left portions of the screen. The F-shaped layout corresponds to the way we naturally read in the West (left to right and top to bottom). A website that is well built will accommodate a reader's natural tendency to scan the page.

V. Visual hierarchy

The grouping of items according to importance is known as visual hierarchy. Size, colour, images, contrast, font, whitespace, texture, and style are some ways to do this. Establishing a focus point is one of the most crucial uses of visual hierarchy since it lets viewers know where the most crucial information is located.

VI. Content

Both outstanding design and amazing content are found on an efficient website. Great content may attract and influence visitors by turning them into clients by using language that is captivating.

VII. Grid based layout

Grids support design organisation and content organisation. The grid makes the page look neat and aligns the elements on the page. A website's appearance is improved by the grid-based layout, which organises content into a neat, rigid grid structure with columns and sections that feel balanced and impose order.

VIII. Load time

A website will lose visitors if you wait for it to load. Nearly half of website visitors anticipate that a page will load in two seconds or less, and they may leave if it takes more than three seconds. Optimizing picture sizes will make your website load more quickly.

IX. Mobile friendly

More people are browsing the web on their phones or other gadgets. It is crucial to think about creating your website with a responsive layout so that it can adapt to various devices.

1.10. PLANNING THE SITE AND NAVIGATION:

The complexity of navigation can range greatly. It may be vertical or horizontal. It can follow you as you scroll down a page or be static. There are no predetermined rules or how-tos for structuring navigation because it might differ so much different websites.

Navigation design is an art form in and of itself, and as designers, we get better at it with practise. Utilizing sound information architecture is crucial:"the art of expressing a model or concept of information used in activities that require explicit details of complex systems."

The greatest navigational layouts and structures will make it as easy as possible for site users to access the material they want to see. If it takes them more than two clicks to reach where they want to go, you run the danger of losing their business entirely.

1.11. Organizing Navigation Structure

The organisation and design of web navigation are arguably the most challenging aspects. After all, programming it may be fairly simple. We'll discuss several techniques and best practises for structuring the navigation in this first section, which can result in a more user-friendly interface and improved conversion rates.

I. Primary vs. Secondary

Most websites require navigation menus, especially those with a lot of content or functionality. However, as a website becomes more complicated, it shouldn't be the sole responsibility of any one menu to direct people to that material and features. No matter how organised it is, all of that stuff simply doesn't always fit in a single, broad menu. Although many websites require more than two, all websites have major and secondary main menus.

The stuff that the majority of people are interested in is designated as primary navigation. However, value varies; on some websites, the same sort of content may be linked from the primary navigation and the secondary navigation (for example, general information about the company or person).

For stuff that only slightly interests the user, there is secondary navigation. This section would house any content that users could still find interesting but does not directly advance the website's main objective. This would typically feature links to "About us," "Contribute," "Advertise," and other pages for many blogs. The client area, FAQ, or support page for other websites may be accessible via the links.

The organisation of the content comes first in the navigation process. You can only decide what is primary and what is secondary once the information has been structured, and only then can you decide where to put any remaining content and how to navigate through it. In alternative menus, whether a submenu, footer menu, sidebar widget, or anyplace else, content that does not match the major or secondary navigation can be placed. Not to imply that primary navigation cannot appear in these locations on the page; there are numerous situations in which drop-down menus or the sidebar make the most sense for primary navigation.

Also, consider whether anything other than the main menu requires navigating. If a supplementary menu is required, why is it so, and how should it be implemented? Regardless of how well organised the content is, if there is a lot of it and you need a more complicated navigational structure, it can be difficult to distinguish between primary and secondary content..

1.12. Grouped content: classification schemes

Another problem comes when a lot of stuff is gathered into one category: what order should it be presented in? To distinguish between top-level and sub-levels of navigation, card sorting and similar techniques may be useful. However, how should the material inside those categories be arranged? Alphabetically? By most utilised or most well-liked? the newest to the oldest?

The most popular content classification techniques are shown here, along with recommendations for their ideal applications.

- Recent to ancient
- Appropriate for timely content.
- Alphabetical
- Excellent when the user needs to locate something quickly. Definitions, indexes, and other items that users are aware of before discovering it are included in this.
- Most widely used or popular
- Excellent for surfing based on interests as opposed to user-required material.
- Geographical
- Is certain content unrelated to some areas or sub-areas?
  - When the steps are taken in order

- The content may be arranged in accordance with the order of steps the user must do if it in any way depicts a process (such as "How to pay your taxes").

I. Common considerations

The main focuses of navigation design are usability and findability. No matter how easy or difficult it is, navigation must be effective for its consumers. We'll now examine several navigational patterns and how these styles may help or hurt websites.

II. Horizontal vs. Vertical

The purpose and design of the website often determine whether to move horizontally or vertically. Most of the time, it's a combination of both, but with primary navigation, we notice some patterns. While major corporate websites frequently employ both horizontal and vertical navigation, small websites frequently use the horizontal navigation at the top of the page (usually with drop-down menus). The principal navigation of blogs can occasionally be horizontal (for pages or categories, for example), while the majority of the other menus are vertical. The navigation on news websites is inconsistent, with no obvious trend in either direction.

The decision to use horizontal navigation as opposed to vertical navigation will be influenced by a number of factors, including design, usability, and content density. To make the navigation stand out more, designers will occasionally add icons or graphic components to the area around it. Rich typography is another typical factor: as the website's navigation is the most visited region, it might receive a specific typographic treatment to enhance and differentiate the user experience.

It would be impossible to put Amazon's departments list into a horizontal menu without it looking crowded. Instead, there is a search bar across the top, which functions as navigation in and of itself. Perhaps significantly more frequently than on other websites, many Amazon shoppers use the search box first because they know exactly what they want. The departmental menu for Amazon is located on the left. The list's primary use is surfing because it is so extensive and diversified, and vertical menus are useful for browsing. The user can narrow down their department and product browsing with the help of the vertical sub-menus.

Simple primary menus should normally be horizontal, however this is not required. Here are a couple layouts that successfully employ vertical menus as the main navigation. A website with a lot of material may quickly overshadow vertical menus, yet all of these websites have straightforward menus and relatively simple designs. The first site down, Good/Corps, is a good illustration of how a lot of information may be presented in a very condensed, even minimalistic style. Users can clearly see the site's hierarchy because subsections are indented.Good/Corps

- Baltic International Bank
- Divensis
- Debbie Millman
- Analogue Digital
- Mellasat
- Cambrian House
- Stura TU-Chemnitz

Of course, horizontal menus can be very effective as well, and best practices-compliant menus don't have to be uninteresting. In fact, it's even possible to combine horizontal and vertical menus.

Below is a brief demonstration of primary or secondary level horizontal menus in use.

- Moody International
- The Big Feastival
- Web Standards Sherpa
- Tijuana Flats
- Unlocking.com
- Cultural Solutions
- Tinkering Monkey
- JustBurns

III. Drop-downs and Mega drop-downs

Larger websites frequently require more in-depth navigation, even though horizontal menus work well for top-level navigation. Drop-down menus can fit a lot of items in one space, thus saving valuable real estate and keeping the navigation organized. The hierarchy can be refined with sub-levels and even sub-levels of sub-levels, helping users filter the information to get to the page or section they want.

Mega drop-downs, which support an even greater diversity of material and layouts, are even more helpful, but more importantly provider larger click areas for users. They can be used to better organize navigation, as well as contain more content while saving space. They are also a great place for additional features and otherwise non-essential content. In both cases it is important to clearly indicate that the drop-down menu is available, either by using arrows or icons or something else.

Here is a brief display:

- Portero Luxury
- Aviary
- Sunglass Hut
- Estee Lauder

Watch how some of these menus cleverly arrange the navigation and content. Here are a few things to remember:

The little showcase's navigation is largely divided into divisions and subcategories.

On many websites, each drop-down menu beneath each top-level link has a separate design and layout. This increases variation and gives the main page of a design the look of subpages.

Some websites feature icons, photos, and regular text for link objects; these components may be utilised for organising, advertising, or just plain usability.

There are a lot more intriguing elements that could be added to the drop-down designs shown above; these are just a few examples. The point is that navigation is sometimes so extensive that sub-menus (whether via drop-downs or mega drop-downs) are necessary.

Unit Summary

We have understood the Protocols and Web Programs related to Web Browser. We have also got introduced to Server and It's Configuration. We have also learnt about Dynamic IP and Web Designing Principles, Planning the site and Navigation

EXERCISE

Multiple Choice Questions

1.1 Expansion of FTP is __________

a) Fine Transfer Protocol

b) File Transfer Protocol

c) First Transfer Protocol

d) Fast Transfer Protocol

1.2 FTP is built on _____ architecture.

a) Client-server

b) P2P

c) Data centric

d) Service oriented

1.3 Which of the following is false with respect to TCP?

a) Connection-oriented

b) Process-to-process

c) Transport layer protocol

d) Unreliable

1.4. TCP process may not write and read data at the same speed. So we need __________ for storage.

a) Packets

b) Buffers

c) Segments

d) Stacks

1.5 To achieve reliable transport in TCP, _________ is used to check the safe and sound arrival of data.

a) Packet

b) Buffer

c) Segment

d) Acknowledgment

1.6 What is a CMS in web design

a) Content Management System

b) Creative Management System

c) Content Mixing System

d) Creatives Managerial System

1.7 Which of the following statements is false

a) You can make a website without using HTML

b) You can make a website without using PHP

c) You can make a website without using CSS

d) You can make a website without using Javascript

1.8 Programs that request data from servers is called

a) users

b) hosts

c) clients

d) programs

1.9 Which of these is not a Web Server?

a) Apache

b) Nginx

c) GWS

d) Chrome

1.10 What services are not a provided by Webservers?

a) Serving Web Pages

b) Running Gateway Programs

c) Resource Sharing

d) Server Side Scripting

Answers to Multiple Choice Questions

1.1 (b) 1.2 (a) 1.3 (d) 1.4 (b) 1.5 (d)1.6 (a) 1.7(a) 1.8 (c) 1.9 (d)1.10(c)

Short and Long Answer Type Questions

Category I

1.1 Explain Different types of Protocols?
1.2 Discuss about Secure Connection
1.3 Explain about Web Server and It's Characteristics

Category II

1.4 Explain Web Development Tools
1.5 Explain in detail about Web Designing principles ?
1.6 Discuss the planning of Web Site Design and Navigation?

References and suggested readings

1. Teach Yourself Java (PROGRAMMING & WEB DEV - OMG) (16 September, 1998) by Joseph O'Neil (Author)
2. Introduction to Networking Protocols and Architecture (wustl.edu)
3. https://amzn.eu/d/4R3Idjv
4. O Level Made Simple – Web Designing & Publishing (M2-R5) by Prof. Satish Jain and M. Geetha Iyer

Dynamic QR CODE for further reading

2 Web Systems Architecture

UNIT SPECIFICS

Through this unit we will discuss the following aspects:

- *Architecture of Web based systems.*
- *Building blocks of fast and scalable data access Concepts.*
- *Load Balancers-queues.*
- *Web Application Architectures.*

RATIONALE

This unit focuses on the Web Application Architecture and the blocks in it such as web page it's types, web browser and web server as well. Understanding the underlying technology, the formats and standards on which the web server is built, as well as the tiers involved in it and the benefits of tiered architecture, is necessary for developing web-models and databases and it's access methods their role in web server architectures and different web component models and its importance in web system architecture

PRE-REQUISITES

Problem Solving Skills

Object Oriented Programming

UNIT OUTCOMES

List of outcomes of this unit is as follows:

U2-O1: Describe the basic Architecture of Web Based Systems

U2-O2: Explain the tiered Architectures of Web Servers

U2-O3: Explain the fast and scalable data access concepts.

U2-O4: Explain the Web Application Architecture.

U2-O5: Apply the Web Application Component Models

Unit-2 Outcomes	EXPECTED MAPPING WITH COURSE OUTCOMES (1- Weak Correlation; 2- Medium correlation; 3- Strong Correlation)				
	CO-1	CO-2	CO-3	CO-4	CO-5
U2-O1	3	3	1	-	-
U2-O2	3	2	2	-	-
U2-O3	3	3	1	2	1
U2-O4	3	3	3	2	1
U2-O5	1	1	3	1	2

2. Architecture of Web Based System:

2.1. Introduction

You will typically use web browser software like Internet Explorer or Mozilla Firefox when you browse the Internet. A client system is a machine running a web browser, whereas a server system is a system that serves up web pages.

Your computer establishes a network connection to a Web Server when you dial up to an Internet Service Provider (ISP). In this case, your computer functions as a client connected to an ISP web server. The web server, as its name implies, provides Web pages to your browser.

"Before understanding the architecture of a web base system let us know about web Browser, web pages, types of web pages, tiers".

2.1.1. Web Browser:

A web browser, also called as a browser, is a piece of software used to access content on the World Wide Web. Chrome, Firefox, Safari, Internet Explorer, Microsoft Edge, opera, and UC Browser are the most widely used browsers. A website is a combination of related web pages hosted on a web server.

2.1.2. Web Page:

A web page is a document on the World Wide Web. In essence, web pages are loaded on web servers and are accessible through a web browser. Text, pictures, audio, video, and hyperlinks can all be found in abundance on a single web page. Links to other web pages can be found in these hyperlinks. The unique Uniform Resource Locator (URL) assigned to each online page, image, and video enables browsers to access these resources from a web server and display them on the user's device.

A reference to a resource on the Internet is made by using a URL, which stands for Uniform Resource Locator.

A URL has two main components
Protocol identifier: http://gmail.com The protocol identifier is http
Resource name: http://gmail.com The resource name is gmail.com

2.1.3. Types of Web Pages:

Based on the response generated by web server web pages are classified into two types

- Static Web Page
- Dynamic Web Page

A. Static Web Page

- Flat or stationary web pages are other names for static web pages.
- The client's browser loads them exactly as they are stored on the web server. These websites solely have static information.
- Users cannot modify or interact with the content; they can only read it.
- HTML and CSS are the only tools used to generate static web pages.
- The information does not need to be changed any more then Static web pages are only utilised

B. Dynamic Web Page

- A dynamic website displays various information at different times.
- A section of a web page can be changed without reloading the complete page..
- Allows to create interactive web pages.

Further dynamic web pages are divided into two categories

- **Server-Side Dynamic Web Page:** This type of web page is produced using server-side scripting. A new web page's construction is based on server-side scripting parameters, which also call for adding more client-side processing.
- **Client-Side Dynamic Web Page:** It is processed using JavaScript or another client-side scripting language. after which it was added to the Document Object Model (DOM).

2.1.4. Tier:

A "layer" is another name for a "tier". The three layers that make up a web-**based system's architecture**

- A presentation layer that communicates with browsers using HTML and CSS. Whether static or dynamically produced, the browser(front-end) will render it. Another name for it is client layer.
- An application layer that executes the application's business logic through the usage of an application server. a server for generation level applications and dynamic content processing. This might have been developed in C#, Java, C++,

Python, Ruby, etc. this is also known as the Logical Layer. Between the Presentation layer and the Database layer, this layer serves as an intermediary. The whole business logic will be written in this layer. It also goes by the name middleware.

- A Data Layer, a database administration tool that gives users access to application data. a database that includes data sets and RDBMS software for managing and accessing the data (back-end). For example, this could be MSSQL, MySQL, or Oracle. It includes methods for connecting to the database and doing necessary operations. Delete, update, etc., are a few examples.

There are many advantages to three-tier design when creating online applications. It gives a developer the chance to modularize, extend, and quickly configure their application.

Example:

As a simple example, to book a movie ticket using web application

i. The presentation layer shows you a web page with some fields, such as the day you want to see the movie and your zip code, for you to fill out.
ii. After the application layer receives this data, it prepares a query and sends it to database layer.
iii. The application layer converts the query results into a web page using the information returned by the database system (a list of movies that are accessible in your area). The presentation layer then shows the page on a laptop or other device when the page is transmitted back to the browser.

2.1.5. The benefits of separating an application into tiers:

i. It enables one tier's technological stack to be updated without affecting other application areas.
ii. It permits separate development teams to focus on their own areas of expertise. Today's engineers are less likely to work on the full stack and are more likely to have significant expertise in one area, such as coding the front end of an application.
iii. The application can be scaled up and out. You can deploy to a range of databases by using a distinct back-end tier, for instance, rather than being restricted to a single technology. You may scale up as well by incorporating additional web servers.
iv. It increases the independence and dependability of the underlying servers or services.

v. It makes the code base easier to maintain by maintaining presentation code and business logic separately so that, for example, a change to business logic won't affect the presentation layer.

2.1.6. The Various Web Based application architecture available are:

1. One-tier architecture
2. Client/Server Two-tier architecture
3. Three-tier architecture

2.1.7. One-tier architecture:

- All the three layers are on the same machine.
- Presentation, Business Logic and Data access logic are tightly connected
- Easy and quick to develop
- Useful for small offices

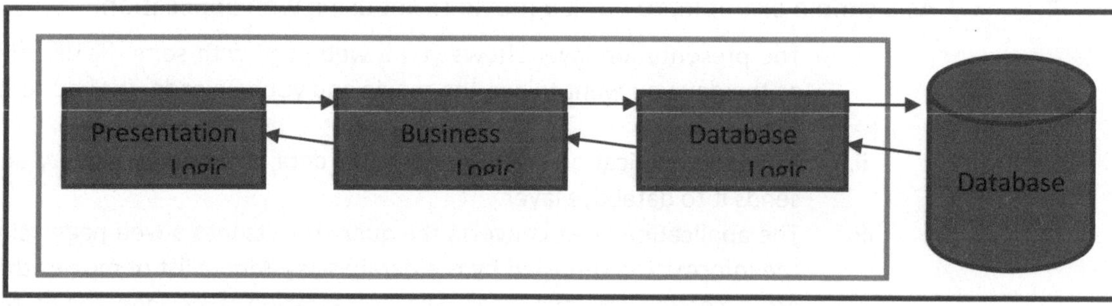

Limitation:

- Tough to update.
- Not scalable. i.e., Tough to increase volume of processing (Scalability)
- Moving to a new machine requires rewriting everything. (Portability)
- Did not protect valuable "Business Logic".
- Changing of one layer needs to change others. (maintenance)

2.1.8. Client/Server (2-tier) Architecture:

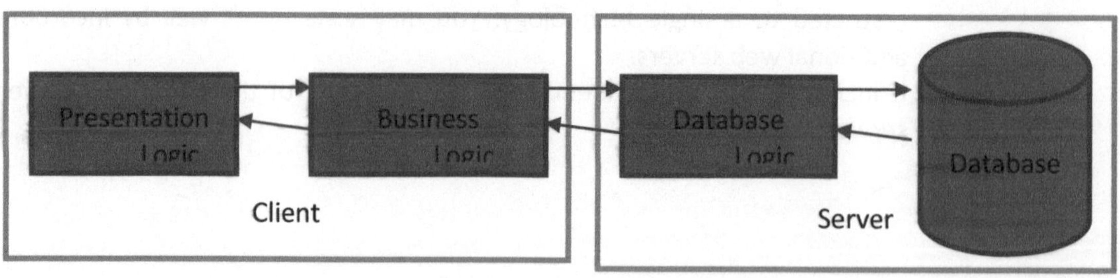

- Database runs on Server.
    - Presentation and logic layers still tightly connected.
    - Protects business logic from UserInterface.

Limitations

- Business-logic is implemented on the Personal Computers
- Increased network traffic
- prevents the reuse of application logic
- necessitates the design and implementation of a protocol for client-server communication.

2.1.9. Three-tier Architecture:

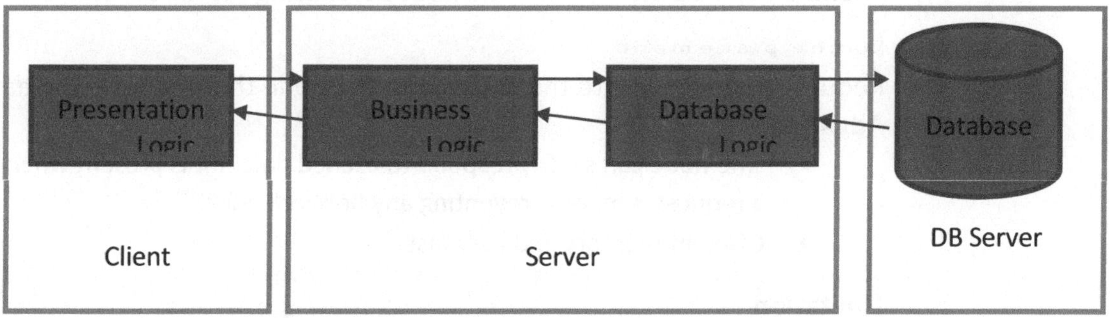

- Each layer might be able to run on a different computer.
- The application logic is clearly separated from user interface control and data presentation.
- Presentation, logic, data layers disconnected
- Modifying the business logic won't require altering the other layers.
- By using of multiple servers Dynamic load balancing is possible
- • Simpler to keep up
- Components can be reused
- Faster development. i.e., Web designer does presentation, software engineer does logic and DB admin does data mode.

2.2. Building blocks of fast and scalable data access Concepts

Most challenging aspect of building web distributed systems is scaling access to the data. While application servers are designed to be stateless and embody a shared-nothing architecture, "the heavy lifting is pushed down the stack to the database server and supporting services." The data access layer is "where the true scaling and performance issues are present.

Caches, proxies, indexes, load balancers, and queues are the building blocks of a scalable data access layer.

2.3. Caches:

Caches are ubiquitous in computing. Their ability to scale read access in a system is clear. They "take advantage of the locality of reference principle: recently requested data is likely to be requested again."

When clients avoid "taxing downstream levels", they enable more growth in the system without the need to scale out. For example, assuming linear scaling and equally taxing requests, if clients implement caching that reduces their usage of the backend by 50%, then the backend can handle twice as many clients without purchasing more resources.

2.3.1. Cache placement

Request Node: collocate the cache with the node *that requests the data*

Advantage

- The node can swiftly respond to cached data if it is present whenever a request is made, preventing any network hops.
- Often in-memory and very fast

Limitation

- When you have multiple request nodes that are load balanced, you may have to cache the same item on all the nodes

2.3.2. Global Cache:

Central cache used by all request nodes

Advantage

- A given item will only be cached only once
- Multiple requests for an item can be collapsed into one request to the backend

Limitation

- Easy to overwhelm a single cache as the number of clients and requests increase

2.3.3. Types

i. **Reverse proxy cache:** cache is responsible for retrieval on cache miss (more common, handles its own eviction)

ii. **Cache as a service:** request nodes are responsible for retrieval on cache miss (typically used when the request nodes understand the eviction strategy or hot spots better than the cache)

iii. **Distributed Cache:** each of the nodes that make up the cache own part of the cached data; divided using a consistent hashing function

Advantage

- Cache space and load capacity can be increased by scaling out (increasing the number of nodes)

Limitation

- Node failure must be handled or intentionally ignored

2.4. Proxies

Proxies are a deceptively simple building block in an architecture: their very nature is to be lightweight, nearly invisible components yet they can provide incredible value to a system by reducing load on the backend servers, providing a convenient location for caching layers, and funnelling traffic appropriately.

2.4.1. Collapsed forwarding

Collapsed forwarding is an example of a technique that proxies can employ to decrease load on a downstream server. In this technique, similar requests are collapsed into a single request that is made to the downstream server; the result of this request is then written to all similar requests, thus reducing the number of requests made.

A simple example of collapsed forwarding is deduplication. If a resource X is requested 100 times, the proxy can make a single request to retrieve X from the downstream server and then write the same response body to the other 99 requests for X.

This is particularly helpful for the downstream server when resource X is large in size. Let's assume a 5 MB payload that must be read into memory (rather than streamed). Without deduplication, the hundred requests would require the server to wastefully read 5 * 99 = 495 MB into memory. The deduplication step in the proxy can smooth over spikes and reduce the memory usage dramatically.

2.4.2. Reverse proxy cache

A reverse proxy cache, as the name implies, is the combination of a proxy and cache. Requests are made to a proxy in front of an origin server which performs best-effort caching. It always reserves the right to fall back on the origin for a definitive response, which is a convenient property that makes failure scenarios relatively straightforward.

A less straightforward problem is handling cache eviction. Let's consider a few options:

- Automatic expiration after a TTL: This option works well with in-memory caches that are intended to protect against spikes of requests. The data isn't cached very long, so its usefulness can be limited, however.
- Intercept modifications and handle evictions: If all modifications to the underlying data go through the proxy layer, the cached data can be evicted as needed.
- Only cache immutable data: In cases where modifications cannot be intercepted or the cached data is a computed result, more advanced techniques must be used. One such technique is to only cache unchanging, immutable data that never becomes stale or needs eviction. While this may seem impractical, it's usually not.

2.5. Indexes

When most developers hear the word "indexes", they immediately jump to database indexes.

Indexes are helpful in the data access layers above the database. Consider a system which is backed by multiple database clusters. Creating an index that maps keys to the database responsible for those keys would eliminate the need to query multiple databases.

2.5.1. Multiple layers of indexes

Once the correct cluster has been identified, another index layer may identify the node within the cluster, and so on. This leads to the point that often-creating multiple layers of indexes is worth the increased write latency. This figure from the chapter illustrates how multiple indexes can guide reads to the correct data:

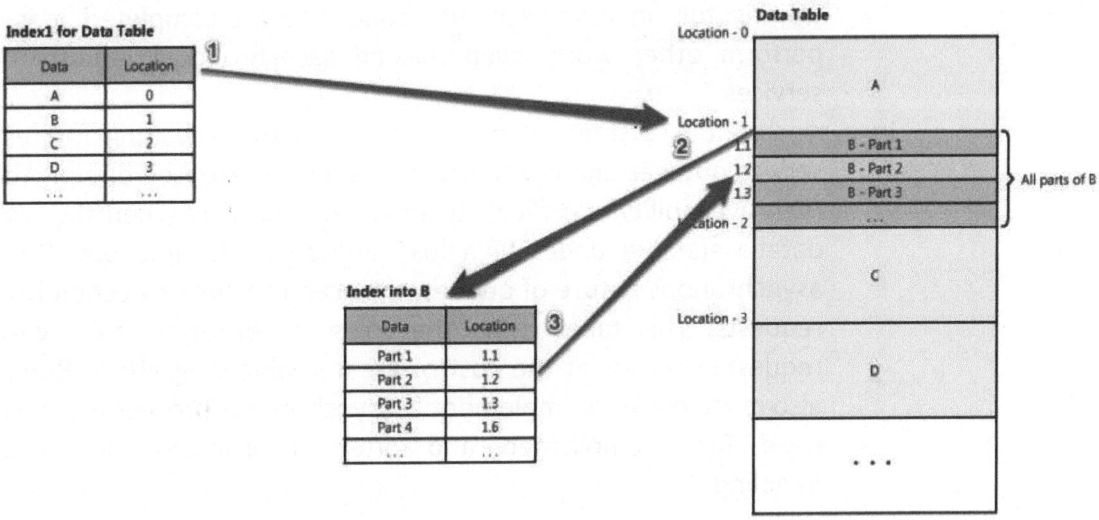

2.5.2. Views

Indexes also allow the same underlying data to be organized differently without resorting to copying through the use of views.

Additionally, indexes can be utilised to generate numerous views of the same data. This is an excellent approach to specify various filters and sorts for huge data sets without having to make numerous additional copies of the data.

2.6. Load balancers

Any architecture must include load balancers since they spread load among a group of nodes in charge of processing requests. This enables various nodes in a system to transparently service the same function.

Like caches, load balancers are placed in many strategic places throughout an architecture. They are also implemented in a variety of ways.

2.7. Queues

Unlike proxies and load balancers which augment an existing architecture and scale reads, queues have a more dramatic impact on the data flow of the architecture and scale writes. Queues have this impact by forcing the introduction of asynchronous processing.

While a synchronous system tightly couples a request to its immediate response, an asynchronous system separates the two. This is achieved by having clients provide a work request to the queue which is not immediately processed while the clients wait. "While the client is waiting for an asynchronous request to be completed it is free to perform other work, even making asynchronous requests of other services."

In a synchronous system where clients are actively waiting for responses, service outages and intermittent failures are exposed directly to clients. High availability is difficult to provide, especially when the underlying database(s) are under high load and requests time out. Due to the asynchronous nature of queues, they can provide protection from failed requests. This takes away the stress of ensuring that every single request succeeds at the cost of great engineering effort. Retry logic is also much easier to implement in asynchronous processing, avoiding the need for "complicated and often inconsistent client-side error handling."

This added protection from a lack of availability in a downstream service and improved retry logic makes a strong argument for the introduction of more queues into an architecture. The client of a queue can often be unaware that a downstream service was temporarily unavailable.

2.8. Web Application architecture (WAA)

The web application architecture outlines how applications, databases, and middleware systems interact over the internet. It ensures that multiple programmes can run simultaneously. To further understand it, let's utilise the basic illustration of opening a website.

An individual web address is requested when a user inserts it into the web browser address bar and clicks Go. In response to the request, the server transmits files to the browser. The files are then run by the browser to display the requested page.

The user can now interact with the website, which is the final step. The code that the web browser has parsed in this case is the most crucial point to remember. Similarly, a web application operates.

The browser may or may not receive precise instructions from this code for how to react to certain user inputs.

The complete software application, in this example a website, must therefore have a web application architecture that includes all of its sub-components as well as external application interchanges.

The web application architecture is essential in the present world since the majority of apps and devices, as well as a significant amount of the global network traffic, rely on web-based communication.

In addition to dealing with efficiency, a web application architecture must also address resilience, scalability, stability, and security.

2.8.1. What is the way it works?

Two distinct programmes (codes) run simultaneously in any typical web application. that are:

i. Code that runs in the browser and reacts to user input is known as **client-side code.**

ii. **Server-side Code** - The server-side programme that replies to HTTP requests

The web developer (team) creating the web application makes the decisions for how the server code will interact with the browser code. C#, Java, JavaScript, Python, PHP, Ruby, and other languages are employed for building server-side programming.

Any programme that has the capacity to reply to HTTP requests is capable of running on a server. The user's requested page is created by the server-side code, which is also in charge of keeping various forms of data, such as user profiles and user input. The end-user never sees it.

The client-side code is created using a combination of CSS, HTML, and JavaScript. The web browser parses this code. Client-side code, as opposed to server-side code, is viewable and modifiable by the user. It responds to input from users.

The client-side code can only access the server through HTTP requests; it cannot directly read files from the server.

2.8.2. Components of web applications

Any of the following two items can be considered web application components:

2.8.2.1. UI/UX Components of Web Application:

Activity logs, dashboards, notifications, settings, analytics, etc. are included in this. These elements have no bearing on how a web application architecture functions. Instead, they are a component of a web app's interface layout strategy.

2.8.2.2. Structural Components

Client and server sides are the two major structural components of a web application

i. Client Component

- The client component is created using JS, CSS, and HTML. There is no requirement for operating system or device-related tweaks because it is already built within the user's web browser. The functionality of a web application is represented by the client component, which the user interacts with.

ii. Server Component

- The frameworks and programming languages like .Net, Java ,NodeJS, PHP, Python, and Ruby on Rails can all be used alone or in combination to create the server component. App logic and database are the two main components of the server. While the latter is where all of the persistent data is saved, the former serves as the web application's primary control centre.

2.8.3. Web applications Component Models:

A web application's model is chosen based on the total servers and databases needed for it. Any one of the following three could be it:

i. One Web Server, One Database

It is both the simplest and least dependable web app component model. Such a model makes use of just one server and one database. As soon as the server goes down, a web app built on such a paradigm will also crash. It is therefore not very trustworthy.

Real web applications rarely use the one server, one database in web application component architecture. In order to study and comprehend the foundations of the web application, it is mostly used for conducting test projects.

ii. One Database, Multiple Web Servers

This type of web application model operates under the premise that the webserver not having data. The database, which is handled outside to the server, is where the webserver writes the information it receives from a client after processing it. On occasion it is also referred to as a stateless architecture.

AICTE'S LIST OF PRESCRIBED TEXTBOOKS

As Per Model Curriculum & Outcome Based Education
aligned with
NATIONAL EDUCATION POLICY 2020

UNDERGRADUATE COURSE BOOKS

S.No.	ISBN	Book Name	Author
1	9789355382160	Advanced Electrical Machines: Theory and Practicals	Bharat Singh Rajpurohit
2	9789355382139	Analog Electronic Circuits: Theory and Practical	Venu Sonti, Sachin Jain
3	9789355383808	Analog Electronic Devices: Theory and Practicals	N. B Balamurugan
4	9789391505158	Basic Electrical Engineering (with Lab Manual)	S.K. Sahdev
5	9789355388087	Basic of Electronics	Brijesh Iyer
6	9789355387127	Basics of Electrical Machines: Theory and Practicals	D. K. Palwalia, U. K. Kalla, R. K. Kumawat
7	9789355389381	Basics of Mechanics	Shubhankar Bhowmick, N. Venkata Swamy Naidu
8	9789355386250	Basics of Thermodynamics	Parmod Kumar, Atul Dhar
9	9789355386984	Biology for Engineers	Annamma Odaneth
10	9789391505141	Chemistry-I	Manisha Agarwal
11	9789355384843	Civil Engineering Societal and Global Impact	Shakuntala Acharya
12	9789355382184	Computer Aided Civil Engineering Drawing	D. Chandra Mouli, B. Swathi
13	9789355382580	Computer Aided Design & Analysis	Hari Kumar Voruganti
14	9789355387592	Computer Architecture	D. Vaithiyanathan
15	9789355385093	Computer Networks	Hari Prabhat Gupta
16	9789355385307	Construction Engineering & Management	Sparsh Johari
17	9789355388728	Control Systems	S.N. Deepa
18	9789355385420	Data Structure and Algorithms	Ranbir Singh Sanasam
19	9789355386700	Design and Analysis of Algorithms	Hari P. Gupta, Rahul Mishra
20	9789355388872	Digital Electronics and System	Abhishek Bhatt
21	9789355386571	Digital Signal Processing	Sanjeev Sharma
22	9789355383396	Disaster management	Pradeep K. Goyal, Anil K. Gupta
23	9789355385222	Discrete Mathematical Structures	Narendra S. Chaudhari, Sharmila S. P.
24	9789355387868	Effective Technical Communication	Pritee Sharma, Sanchita Verma
25	9789355383389	Electrical Circuit Analysis and Network Theory	Shouri Chatterjee
26	9789355388957	Electromagnetic Waves	Uttam M. Pal, Srijith K.
27	9789355384652	Electronic Communication	Vimal Bhatia
28	9789355388711	Embedded Systems	Santanu Chattopadhyay
29	9789355385147	Energy Science and Engineering	M. Rizwan, Majid Jamil
30	9789355387929	Engineering Economics, Estimation & Costing	Yogesh C. Joshi
31	9789355384669	Engineering Geology	R. N. Khare, Ketan Chourasia
32	9789391505066	Engineering Graphics & Design	Pradeep Jain
33	9789391505097	English (with Lab Manual)	Kulbhushan Kumar
34	9789355385963	Environmental Engineering	Chandra Sekhar Matli
35	9789355388117	Fluid Mechanics	Shreenivas N. Londhe, Pradnya R. Dixit
36	9789355388377	Fluid Mechanics & Fluid Machines	R.P. Saini
37	9789355387103	Geotechnical Engineering	Paramita Bhattacharya

UNDERGRADUATE COURSE BOOKS

S.No.	ISBN	Book Name	Author
38	9789355385130	Hydraulic Engineering	Sayantan Ganguly
39	9789355385550	Hydrology & Water Resources Engineering	Mitthan Lal Kansal, P.K. Agarwal
40	9789355389688	Information Technology Workshop in MATLAB	Hari Prabhat Gupta
41	9789355383235	Instrumentation for Civil Engineering Applications	Ashim Kanti Dey, Manita Das
42	9789355387042	Introduction to Civil Engineering	Manabendra Saharia, Nagendra R. Velaga
43	9789355384805	Introduction to Database Systems	Vikram Singh
44	9789355387509	Machine Element & System Design	Sabah Khan
45	9789355385383	Machine Learning	Himanshu Mittal
46	9789355388414	Manufacturing Automation	Chitragupt Swaroop Chitransh
47	9789355387233	Manufacturing Processes	Dheerendra Kumar Dwivedi
48	9789355389886	Materials Engineering	Dheerendra Kumar Dwivedi
49	9789391505172	Mathematics - I Calculus and Linear Algebra [For Non-Computer Science Engineering Branches]	Reena Garg
50	9789391505271	Mathematics - I Calculus and Linear Algebra [For Computer Science Engineering Branches]	Reena Garg
51	9789355384607	Measurements & Metrology	V.P. Chandramohan
52	9789355383730	Mechanics of Materials	Arvind Vyavahare
53	9789355383358	Mechatronics, Robotics & Control	J. Srinivas
54	9789355385116	Microprocessor and Microcontroller	Saurabh Chaudhury, Risha Mal
55	9789355386083	Microprocessors	Yogendra Kumar Gupta
56	9789355389169	Mobile Communication and Networks	Vimal Bhatia
57	9789355385475	Operating Systems	Sukomal Pal
58	9789355385604	Operating Systems	Sanjaya Kumar Panda
59	9789391505134	Physics (Oscillations, Waves and Optics) With lab manual	A.B. Bhattacharya, Atanu Nag
60	9789391505257	Physics (Quantum Mechanics for Engineers) With lab manual	A.B. Bhattacharya, Atanu Nag
61	9789391505165	Physics (Introduction to Electromagnetic Theory) (with Lab Manual)	A.B. Bhattacharya, Atanu Nag
62	9789391505059	Physics (Introduction to Mechanics) (with Lab Manual)	A.B. Bhattacharya, Atanu Nag
63	9789355385956	Power Electronics: Theory and Practicals	Lalit Chandra Saikia
64	9789355384942	Power Systems-I	Suresh Mikkili
65	9789355386236	Power Systems-II	Arun Rahul S, Manas K. Jena
66	9789355383754	Product Innovation & Entrepreneurship	Vigneswaran C
67	9789355384584	Production & Operation Management	Navin Kumar Dev
68	9789391505219	Programming for Problem Solving (with Lab Manual)	R.S. Salaria
69	9789355385451	Signals and Systems	Sanjay L. Nalbalwar
70	9789355386021	Strength of Materials	Uday Shanker Dixit, Nelson Muthu, S. M. Kamal
71	9789355383792	Structural Engineering	T.D. Gunneswara Rao, D. Ravi Prasad
72	9789355387004	Surveying and Geomatics	P. K. Garg
73	9789355384317	Testing & Evaluation of Civil Engineering Materials	Sandeep Chaudhary, Kashyap A Patel
74	9789355382306	Theory of Computation	Debi Prasanna Acharjya
75	9789355384928	Transportation Engineering	A.K. Raji
76	9789355385208	VLSI Design	Mahendra Sakare, Shonal Chouksey
77	9789391505332	Workshop / Manufacturing Practices (with Lab Manual)	Veeranna D.K.

DIPLOMA COURSE BOOKS

S.No.	ISBN	Book Name	Author
1	9789355382481	Aanandam An Act of Community Service	Shuchi Sharma
2	9789355385567	Advanced Manufacturing Processes	Ranjeet Kumar Sahu, Devendra Laxman Kamble
3	9789355385109	Advanced Surveying: Theory & Practice	Ramakant Agrawal, Parshottam Sarathe
4	9789355384546	Algorithms	Piyoosh P, Arnab Sarkar
5	9789391505448	Applied Chemistry (with Lab Manual)	Anju Rawlley, Devdatta Vinayakrao Saraf
6	9789391505431	Applied Physics-I (with Lab Manual)	Vinod Kumar Yadav, Mina Talati
7	9789391505578	Applied Physics-II (with Lab Manual)	Hussain Jeevakhan
8	9789355387530	Basic Mechanical Engineering	Dharmendra Singh, Chandra Shekhar Rajoria
9	9789355387394	Building Construction	Rinku Kumar, Sandeep Panchal
10	9789355383280	Building Electrification	Arnab Ghosh
11	9789355384379	Building Planning and Drawing	Aparna Dwivedi
12	9789391505493	Communication Skills in English	Anjana Tiwari
13	9789355383570	Computer Aided Machine Drawing Practice	Kanak Kalita
14	9789355388964	Computer Networking and Data Communication	Sanjaya Shankar Tripathy
15	9789355382986	Computer Networks: Theory & Practicals	Brijendra Pratap Singh, Manoj Madhava Gore
16	9789355382672	Computer Programming: Theory and Practicals	Satyendra Singh Chouhan
17	9789355387714	Computer System Organization	Sonal Yadav
18	9789355382658	Concrete Technology: Theory and Practice	Sasankasekhar Mandal, Vishwajit Anand, Sushil K. Agarwala
19	9789355383334	Construction Materials and Testing	Vanita Aggarwal
20	9789355383501	Consumer Electronics	Amit M. Joshi, Maulin M. Joshi, Urvashi Prakash Shukla
21	9789355387684	Data Structures: Theory & Practicals	NB Venkateswarlu
22	9789355388513	Design of Machine Elements	A. Kumaravel, M. Kathirselvam
23	9789355388360	Design of Steel and RCC Structure	Sparsh Johari
24	9789355383303	Digital Communication	Muralidhar Kulkarni, K. S. Shivaprakasha
25	9789355387295	Digital Electronics	Menka Yadav
26	9789355389435	Electric Circuits and Networks	Jamuna K., Nilanjan Tewari
27	9789355388452	Electric Motors and Transformers (Theory and Practicals)	Sanjay B. Bodkhe
28	9789355385901	Electric Power Transmission and Distribution	Sudhir Sharma
29	9789355389466	Electrical & Electronics Measurements and Instrumentation	Sudarsan Sahoo, Vipin Chandra Pal, Sudipta Chakraborty
30	9789355382696	Electronic Communication	M. D. Selvaraj, P. Nagaradjane
31	9789355387202	Electronic Devices and Circuits	Ankesh Jain
32	9789355386373	Electronic Equipment Maintenance	Chanchal Sharma
33	9789355384690	Embedded Systems	Deepa M, G. Santhanamari, Susithra. N
34	9789355384867	Energy Conservation and Audit	M. Rizwan, Majid Jamil
35	9789391505509	Engineering Graphics	Sharad K. Pradhan, K.K. Jain
36	9789391505608	Engineering Mechanics (with Lab Manual)	Bhankhar Bharat, Gokaldas Vandana Somkuwar

DIPLOMA COURSE BOOKS

S.No.	ISBN	Book Name	Author
37	9789391505516	Engineering Workshop Practice	A. K. Sarathe
38	9789391505653	Environmental Science	Subrat Roy
39	9789355384966	Estimating, Costing and valuation	Sandeep Panchal
40	9789355389510	Fluid Mechanics & Hydraulic Machinery	Suman Chakraborty, Sourav Mitra, Aditya Bandopadhyay
41	9789391505592	Fundamentals of Electrical and Electronics Engineering (with Lab Manual)	Susan S. Mathew, Saji T. Chacko
42	9789355387240	Fundamentals of Power Electronics	Soumitra Kumar Mandal
43	9789355389602	Geotechnical Engineering (Theory & Practicals)	Neelima Satyam
44	9789355386137	Induction, Synchronous, and Special Electrical Machines	K. Selvajyothi, S. Tamilselvi, Sarat Kumar Sahoo
45	9789355382290	Industrial Engineering & Management	A. Manimaran
46	9789355384959	Internet of Things	Sujata Pal
47	9789355388650	Introduction to DBMS: Theory & Practicals	Myneni Madhu Bala
48	9789355384294	Introduction to e-Governance	Kamal Kant Verma
49	9789355386564	Introduction to Electric Generation Systems	Lalit Chandra Saikia, Nalin Behari, Deb Choudhury
50	9789391505585	Introduction to IT Systems (with Lab Manual)	Prashant Joshi
51	9789355382900	Linear Integrated Circuit	B. T. Krishna
52	9789355388148	Manufacturing Engineering	Santosh Kumar
53	9789355383877	Material Science & Engineering	Vinod Kumar, Nisheeth k. Prasad
54	9789391505424	Mathematics-I	Deepak Singh
55	9789391505523	Mathematics-II	Garima Singh
56	9789355385994	Measurements and Metrology	A. Gnanavelbabu, M. Santhana kumar, R. Saranraj
57	9789355388131	Mechanics of Materials and their Testing	R. Velmurugan, Pragathi
58	9789355385048	Microcontroller Applications	Ritula Thakur
59	9789355385062	Microcontrollers and Applications	Santanu Chattopadhyay
60	9789355388100	Mobile and Wireless Communication	Maulin Joshi, Urvashi P. Shukla
61	9789355387790	Production & Operations Management	Mayank Kumar Agrawal
62	9789355388704	Public Health Engineering	Rinku Kumar
63	9789355387455	Python Programming	Rupesh Nasre
64	9789355387189	Renewable Energy Technologies	Sanjay Agrawal, Rajeev K. Mishra
65	9789355387479	Software Engineering	Salman Abdul Moiz
66	9789355389749	Theory of Machines & Mechanisms	G. C. Mohan Kumar
67	9789355387332	Theory of Structures	Arunachalam Subramanian Balu
68	9789355389015	Thermal Engineering - I	V. Raghavan
69	9789355389831	Thermal Engineering - II	Parvesh Antil
70	9789355386779	Transportation Engineering (Theory & Practice)	A.K. Raji, K.K. Babu
71	9789355384287	Water Resource Engineering (Theory & Practice)	Prakash C. Swain, Dillip K. Ghose
72	9789355383051	Web Technologies: Theory & Practical	Raman Dugyala

BOOKS ARE ALSO AVAILABLE IN

HINDI | MARATHI | TAMIL | BENGALI | GUJARATI

Also available as an ebook

For Detailed Catalogue, Please Scan QR Code

This web application component model needs at least two web servers. It's everything to prevent failure. One of the web servers can still function while the other takes over.

All incoming requests will be instantly sent to the new server, where the web application will continue to run. As a result, the server with implicit database is less reliable. But if the database fails, the web application will also fail.

iii. Multiple Web Servers and Databases

Due to the lack of a single point of failure in the webservers or databases, it is the most effective component model for online applications. For this kind of model, there are two choices. to evenly distribute data throughout all active databases, or to ensure consistency between them.

For the former, normally no more than 2 databases are needed, however for the latter, in the event of a database crash, some data may become unavailable. But in both cases, DBMS normalisation is applied.

When the scale is big Installing load balancers is, such as when there are more than 5 web servers, databases or both.

2.8.4. The Architecture Types of Web Application:

An interaction pattern between different web application components is known as a web application architecture. How the application functionality is split between the client and server sides determines the type of web application architecture.

The web application architecture majorly contains three main forms. The following is an explanation of each of them:

i. Single-Page Apps (SPAs)

Single page web applications allow for dynamic interaction by updating material on the currently shown page rather than downloading new pages from the server each time a user takes a step.

AJAX, a condensed version of asynchronous JavaScript and XML, is the building block that makes page communications possible and, in turn, makes SPAs a possibility. Because they avoid user interruptions, single-page applications resemble traditional desktop applications in several aspects.

The majority of the necessary content and information elements are requested by SPAs because of the way they were designed. As a result, an intuitive and engaging user experience is acquired.

ii. **Microservices**

These are little, lightweight services that carry out just one function. With the help of the Microservices Architecture framework, developers may increase productivity and hasten the deployment process overall.

The parts of an application created with the Microservices Architecture are not reliant on one another. As a result, using the same programming language to create them is not necessary.

So, when working with the Microservices Architecture, developers are allowed to use any technology stack they like. It facilitates and speeds up application development.

iii. **Serverless Architectures**

An application developer consults a third-party cloud infrastructure services provider in this form of web application architecture to outsource server and infrastructure administration.

This method has the advantage of letting applications run code logic without having to worry about equipment-related activities.

The Serverless Architecture works best in situations where the web application development company does not want to handle or support the servers in addition to the hardware.

2.9. Advice for Web App Development:

Web application that is operational cannot be referred to as "the finest." A web application must be more than just functional to be considered outstanding.

Numerous considerations should be made during the construction of a web application to guarantee that it can deliver the best performance possible.

Web application must:

- Prevent frequent collisions
- Have the flexibility to scale up or down.
- Be easy to use
- Be able to react more quickly
- Implement automatic Installations

- Error Logs
- Not contain any points of failure.
- Provide a consistent and uniform response to the question.
- Adherence to the most recent standards and technologies
- Increased security measures should be used to reduce the likelihood of harmful intrusions.

Unit Summary

Through this unit we have understood the Architecture of Web based systems and Building blocks of fast and scalable data access Concepts. We have also learnt about the Load Balancers-queue and Web Application Architectures.

EXERCISE

Multiple Choice Questions

1.1 A ________ web page is not interactive and is used to display information only.

a) Dynamic
b) Static
c) Server
d) Client

1.2 A ________ web page is not interactive and is used to display information only.

a) Dynamic
b) Static
c) Server
d) Client

1.3 The background color of a Web page is determined by the ______ property.

a) BackColor
b) BackgroundColor
c) BgColor
d) BColor

1.4. A ________ is a special computer that serves webpages.

a) Server
b) Host
c) Client
d) Router

1.5 A _______ computer requests web pages from the server.

a) Server

b) Host

c) Client

d) Router

1.6 _______ is used to convert your application into Web-Application.

a) Struts Services

b) Web Services

c) Java Service

d) Browser Action

1.7 The basic Web Services platform is combination of _____ and _______

a) CSS + HTTP

b) XML + HTML

c) XML + HTTP

d) CSS + JAVA

1.8 What type of protocol is HTTP?

a) stateless

b) stateful

c) transfer protocol

d) information protocol

1.9 What does MIME stand for?

a) Multipurpose Internet Messaging Extension

b) Multipurpose Internet Mail Extension

c) Multipurpose Internet Media Extension

d) Multipurpose Internet Mass Extension

1.10 How can we take input text from user in HTML page?

a) input tag

b) inoutBufferedReader tag

c) meta tag

d) scanner tag

Answers to Multiple Choice Questions

1.2 (b) 1.2 (a) 1.3 (c) 1.4 (a) 1.5 (c)1.6 (b) 1.7(c) 1.8 (a) 1.9 (b)1.10(a)

Short and Long Answer Type Questions

Category I

1.1 What is a tier in terms of Web Architecture?
1.2 What is the role of web Browser in web Applications?
1.3 Define Cache?
1.4 Write about types of web pages

Category II

1.5 Explain three tier Architecture?
1.6 Explain in detail about Web Development tools ?
1.7 Discuss about Web Services?
1.8 Explain Web applications Component Models?
1.9 Discuss about proxies and indexes in web applications architecture ?

References and suggested readings

1. Web Components in Action by Ben Farrell Foreword by Gray Norton August 2019 ISBN 9781617295775 432 pages
2. What is Web Application Architecture? Components, Models, and Types (hackr.io)https://amzn.eu/d/4R3Idjv
3. Web Application Architecture: Principles, Protocols and Practices 1st Edition by Leon Shklar (Author), Rich Rosen (Author)
4. Web Application Architecture: Components, Models, and Types (scnsoft.com)

Dynamic QR CODE for further reading

3 Java Script Introduction

UNIT SPECIFICS

Through this unit we will discuss the following aspects:

- *Client-side Scripting.*
- *Building blocks of java Scripts.*
- *Functions in Java Script.*
- *Loops and repetition.*

RATIONALE

This unit completely focuses on the Introduction to JavaScript. It basically deals with client-side scripting and its importance in web applications. It also deals with definition of java script and it's characteristics, features and the limitations as well. How to embed java script in HTML java script types such as External script and Internal script, the various function blocks like variables, keywords, comments, conditional statements and operators too. The unit also covers arrays and functions.

PRE-REQUISITES

Problem Solving Skills

Object Oriented Programming

UNIT OUTCOMES

List of outcomes of this unit is as follows:

U3-O1: Explain the Client-Side Programming

U3-O2: Explain the introductory concepts of Script

U3-O3: Explain the Constructs of Java Script.

U3-O4: Explain the arrays in Java Script.

U3-O5: Apply the functions in Java Script

Unit-3 Outcomes	EXPECTED MAPPING WITH COURSE OUTCOMES (1- Weak Correlation; 2- Medium correlation; 3- Strong Correlation)				
	CO-1	CO-2	CO-3	CO-4	CO-5
U3-O1	2	2	3	-	2
U3-O2	1	1	3	1	2
U3-O3	2	2	3	1	2
U3-O4	2	2	3	1	2
U3-O5	1	1	3	1	2

3. Dynamic HTML (DHTML):

Dynamic HTML (DHTML) provides different technologies required to make webpages dynamic and HTML.

DHTML is a combination of HTML, CSS & Scripting languages (Java Script) and DOM.

- CSS – Allows to control style & layout of webpages
- JavaScript – Used to control access and manipulate HTML elements.
- DOM – Document object model, defines a standard set of object for HTML.

3.1. Client side scripting:

- Script code written on client. (Browser)
- It is performed to generate a code that can run on the client end (Browser) without needing the server side processing.
- Script is placed inside the HTML document.
- Used to examine the user's form for the errors before submitting it.
- The effective client-side scripting can significantly reduce the server load.
- Client-side scripting requires browsers to run the scripts on the client machine but does not interact with the server while processing the client-side scripts.
- HTML, CSS, JavaScript, Jscript, VB Script etc are client – side scripting languages.
- The client-side script executes the code to the client side which is visible to the users.

3.2. JavaScript:

- A script is a program code written using a Scripting language.

- A scripting language is a kind of programming language with less functionality. Eg: JavaScript, VBscript, ASP, PHP.
- JavaScript is interpreted; client-side and object based scripting language that offers to create dynamic and interactive webpages.
- HTML & JavaScript applications can be developed on Microsoft Front-page, Macromedia Dreamweaver, and macromedia Himesite5.

3.2.1. JavaScript Characteristics:

- JavaScript is standardized by "European Computer manufacture association" (ECMA), also called ECMA Script.
- Originally named "Live Script", developed by Netscape & Sun Microsystems
- It is a Client-side Scripting language, the Scripts run in the browser.
- The script is processed by line by line, hence it is interpreted language.
- The script engine (interpreter) is a built-in component of the web browser.
- It is a Case Sensitive language.
- Uses control statements, events and in-built objects to make webpages dynamic.
- Used to develop interactive and dynamic webpages.
- It is relatively simple to learn & implement.
- It is reduces demand on server as it is a client-side scripting language.
- Variables need not to be declared before their use.
- Checking the compatibility of type can be done dynamically.
- Java script objects are dynamic. i.e, Allows changing data and methods of an object during execution.
- JavaScript is used to validate the data on the webpage before submitting it to the server. i.e. "Client- side validation".
- JavaScript is an untyped language. i.e. a variable can hold any type of value.
- JavaScript is a free formed language. i.e. no constraints on spacing, line breaks etc.

3.2.2. Limitations:

- JavaScript does not allow reading or writing of files (For Security Reason).
- Not support to develop network applications.
- Doesn't have any multithreading or multiprocessor capabilities.

3.2.3. Features of JavaScript:

- All browsers support java scripting, no need to use any plug-in.
- Uses structured programming language syntax. (similar to c/c++)
- No need to place semicolon (;) at the end of statement.
- Data type is bound to the value and not to the variable. Hence it is untyped language
- Using"eval" functions, the expression can be evaluated at runtime.
- Provide built-in objects.
- Supports use of regular expressions using which text-pattern matching is done. Used to validate webpage data.
- It is a function programming. i.e. supports functions.
- Light weight programming language for network- centric applications.
- Less server interaction. i.e. validates user input before sending the page to server.
- Immediate feedback to the user
- Provides rich set of interfaces like popup windows, drag & drop components.
- Effective event handing mechanism.

3.3. Embedding JavaScript in HTML page:

- The script is embedded in HTML document using <SCRIPT> tag.
- The browser process the script code in <script> tag.
- The attributes of <script> tag are
    - **type** – The type can be "text/JavaScript"
    - **language** – The attribute can have value " javascript" or "vbscript".
    - **src** – URL of the script file for embedding. Used for external script files.

3.3.1. The script can be

I. **Inline script / Embedded script**

The script code is specified in the HTML document using <SCRIPT> tag in <HEAD>/<BODY>

Example:

```
<html>
<head>
```

```
<script     type     =     "text/javascript">
    document.write("Welcome to javascript")
</script>
</head>
<body> </body>
<html>
```

II. External script

The javascript code is stored in a separate file using ".js" extension.

Eg: s cript.js

document.write("External script"); document.write("<BR>");
document.write("Welcome to Javascript");

The script file can be accessed in a webpage using <script> tag

Example:

```
<html>
<head>
<script                               src='script.js"
    type="text/javascript">
</script>
</head>
<body>
<H1> JavaScript </H1>
</body>
</html>
```

3.3.2. Reserved Words/keywords

break	*case*	*catch*	*return*	*type of*
continue	*default*	*do*	*switch*	*with*
delete	*else*	*finally*	*this*	*var*
for	*function*	*if*	*throw*	*void*
in	*instance of*	*new*	*try*	*while*

3.3.3. JavaScript Comments

- Single line comments //comment line appear here
- Multiline comments /* comments in multiple lines will appear here */
- XHTML based comments <! – comments here //-->

3.3.4. Variables in JavaScript

- Variables are named locations in the memory and used to store data.
- A variable has name, value and memory address, "var" keyword is used to declare a variable

- JavaScript allows dynamic initialization. i.e. variable can be declared when it is needed.
- Keywords cannot be used for variable names.
  Example: var no, name, avg;

```
var x;
var sum = 0;
-----
Ex: var x = 10; // integer type - x
          X = "hello" // x is string type
          X = 13.45 // x is float type.
```

A variable in JavaScript can hold any type of value. The particular type is known dynamically during last assignment. "Hence JavaScript "is untyped language.

3.4. Control Statements:

- Conditional statements
- If, if-else, nested if, else-if ladder,
- switch. (Case constant can be 'string' also).
- loop/Iterative statements while, do while, for.
- Jump statements Break, continue.

3.5. Operator in JavaScript

Arithmetic operators – `+,-,*,|, %, ++,--`

Assignment operators – `=, +=,-=,*=,|=, %=`

Comparison operators – `==, =,>, >=, <, <=`

Logical operators – `&&, ||,!`

Conditional operators – `?:x=(a<b), a:b;`

Special operators – `type of`

The precedence of operators is

```
!, -, ++, --, typeof
*, |, %
+, -
<, <=, >, >=
```

```
==, !=
&&, ||, ?:
=,+=, -=, *=, |=, %=
```

The scope of variables can be local to the block, function and global.

3.6. Arrays in JavaScript

- An array is a named collection of different values. The individual values are represented by their respective array elements, each of which has a unique index.
- In JavaScript, arrays are instances of the "Array "object.
- Arrays are dynamic, defined or created using "new" keyword. In JavaScript the values in an array need not to be of same data type.
  Ex: An array can have both integer and string values.

```
var  arr_name  =  new
    Array(size); var
    arr_name  =  new
    Array(size); var
    arr_name  =  new
    Array();
```

Example:

```
var a = new
  Array(10);
var list = new
    Array();
```

An array can be initialized as

```
var marks = new Array (30, 40, 50, 60);
var data = new Array (530," D. Raman",8.9);
```

A particular element of an array can be accessed by specifying index. (Starts with 0). In JavaScript array a place holder can be specified to add/insert element later.

Example: var marks = new Array (10, 20, 40, 50);

Later marks [2] = 80;

3.7. Function in JavaScript

A function refers to a cohesive bluck of statements that has a name and can be accessed or called from anywhere and any number of times in the script.

The function can be defined as

```
Function fun_name (par1, par2 … parN)
  {
  //     function     statements
       [Return expn]
  }
```

- A function can have zero or more parameters.
- A function may or may not return a value.

Example:

```
function add (a, b, c)
    {
        var avg = (a+b+c)/3;
        return avg;
    }
```

The function can be called as **var y = add (10, 20, 30);**

3.7.1. Built in functions of JavaScript

I. alert () –

- Used to display information a pop up box/ message box. (dialog)
- Used to display error messages once a form is validated.
- Defined in "window "object.
  window.alert ("message"); or alert ("message");

  Example: `window.alert ("enter a valid phone no");`

II. prompt () –

- displays a message box containing a text box with OK & Cancel Buttons
- It returns a text string when OK is clicked and null when cancel is

clicked. Used to accept input data from the user for script code.

- defined in "windows" object.

  window.prompt ("message", "default value"); or window.prompt ("message");

  Example: `var no = window.prompt ("enter a no", "o"); var no = prompt ("enter a no");`

III. **Confirm () –**

- display a dialog box with two buttons OK & Cancel. When OK is clicked, returns true otherwise returns false.
- Used to take user confirmation.
- defined in "windows" object.

  window.confirm ("would you like to do?"); or confirm ("message here");

  Example: window.confirm("save or not ?");

IV. **isFinite () –**

- checks whether a value is finite or not.
- Returns true if the argument is a finite value.

  Var isFinite (arg)

  Example: var x = isFinite (204);
  document.writeln (x); //true.

V. **isNaN () –**

- checks whether a value is number or not.
- (NaN) --> Not a number.
- returns true if the argument is string,

  isNaN (arg);

  Example: var x = isNaN ("welcome"); //true
  var y = isNaN ("2022"); //false

VI. **ParseInt () –**

- It parses the string and returns the first integer value found in the string.

  ParseInt(string);

Example: var x = parseInt("2022"); //2022
var y = parseInt("welcome");// NaN "Return NaN if it is not a no".

VII. parseFloat () –

- Parse the string and returns the first float value found in the string.
  ParseFloat(string);
  Example: var x = parseFloat ("2022"); //2022
  var y = parseFloat ("welcome");// NaN "Return NaN if it is not a no".

VIII. eval () –

- It accepts a string containing JavaScript code, evaluates the argument and returns the resulting value.
  eval(string);
  Example: eval (" x = 50; y = 10;

  document.write(x+y)"); //Gives => 60.

  document.write(eval("10*5")); //50

  var x = 50; document.writeln (eval(x/3));

  var x = eval ("104/3");

IX. Number () –

- Used to convert the value of an object into a number.
  Example: var x = Number (Boolean (true)); //1
  var y = Number (String ("1998")); //1998
  var z = Number (String ("wel done")); //NaN

3.7.2. Primitive Data types

Float	Integer / Number	Null
String	Boolean	Undefined

Unit Summary

Through this unit we have larnt about the Client-side Scripting and Building blocks of java Scripts. We have also understood the key concepts viz., Functions in Java Script Loops and repetition.

EXERCISE

Multiple Choice Questions

1.1 DHTML is a combination of _________ and __________.

a) DOM and CSS

b) CSS and Conventional HTML

c) HTML and JavaScript

d) None of the above

1.2 Which type of JavaScript language is ___

a) Object-Oriented

b) Object-Based

c) Assembly-language

d) High-level

1.3 The "function" and " var" are known as:

a) Keywords

b) Data types

c) Declaration statements

d) Prototypes

1.4. Which one of the following is the correct way for calling the JavaScript code?

a) Pre-processor

b) Triggering Event

c) RMI

d) Function/Method

1.5 Which of the following type of a variable is volatile?

a) Mutable variable

b) Dynamic variable

c) Volatile variable

d) Immutable variable

1.6 In JavaScript the x===y statement implies that:

a) Both x and y are equal in value, type and reference address as well.

b) Both are x and y are equal in value only.

c) Both are equal in the value and data type.

d) Both are not same at all.

1.7 In JavaScript, what will be used for calling the function definition expression:

a) Function prototype
b) Function literal
c) Function calling
d) Function declaration

1.8 Which one of the following is used for the calling a function or a method in the JavaScript:

a) Property Access Expression
b) Functional expression
c) Invocation expression
d) Primary expression

1.9 Which one of the following operator is used to check weather a specific property exists or not:

a) Exists
b) exist
c) within
d) in

1.10 Which one of the following is an ternary operator:

a) ?
b) :
c) -
d) +

Answers to Multiple Choice Questions

1.3 (c) 1.2 (a) 1.3 (c) 1.4 (a) 1.5 (c)1.6 (b) 1.7(b) 1.8 (c) 1.9 (d)1.10(a)

Short and Long Answer Type Questions

Category I

1.1 Explain Embedding Java Script in HTML?
1.2 Write the characteristics of Java Script?
1.3 List the features of Java Script?

Category II

1.4 Discus the types of Java Script?
1.5 Explain arrays in Java Script?
1.6 Explain functions in Java Script?

PRACTICE:

Programs on JavaScript Control Statements, Arrays and Functions

<!-- Greatest of 2 numbers -->

```
<!doctype html>
<html lang="en">
<head>
<title>if-else statement</title>
<script language="javascript"
    type="text/javascript" >
    var a = window.prompt("Enter a number", "0");
    a = parseInt(a);
    var b= parseInt(prompt("Enter b number"));
    if(a > b)
     window.alert("The greatest is " +a);
    else
     alert("The greatest is " +b);
</script>
</head>
<body>
</body>
</html>
```

<!-- Arranging 3 numbers in order -->

```
<!doctype html>
<html lang="en">
<head>
<title>nested if statement</title>
</head>
```

```
<body>
<script language="javascript" type="text/javascript" >
    var a = parseInt(window.prompt("Enter Marks Sub1"));
    var b= parseInt(prompt("Enter Marks Sub2"));
    var c= parseInt(prompt("Enter Marks Sub3"));
    var avg=(a+b+c)/3;
    if(avg >= 70)
      alert("First With Distinction");
      else if(avg >=60 && avg <70) alert("First Class");
      else if(avg >=50 && avg <60) alert("Second Class");
      else if(avg >=40 && avg <50) alert("Third Class");
      else alert("Fail");
</script>
</body>
</html>
```

<!-- Arranging 3 numbers in order -->

```
<!doctype html>
<html lang="en">
<head>
<title>nested if statement</title>
<script  language="javascript"  type="text/javascript"  >
    var a = parseInt(window.prompt("Enter a number", "0"));
    var b= parseInt(prompt("Enter b number"));
    var c= parseInt(prompt("Enter c number"));
    if(a <b && a<c)
      {
      if(b < c)
           document.writeln("The order is " +a+ "," +b+","+c);
      else
           document.writeln("The order is " +a+ "," +c+","+b);
      }
    else
      if(b<a && b<c)
          {
           if(a <c)
```

```
            document.writeln("The order is " +b+ "," +a+","+c);
             else
            document.writeln("The order is " +b+ "," +c+","+a);
            }
      else
            {
            if(b <a)
             document.writeln("The order is " +c+ "," +b+","+a);
            else
             document.writeln("The order is " +c+ "," +a+","+b);
            }
</script>
</head>
<body>
</body>
</html>
```

<!—Arithmetic operations using switch -->

```
<!doctype html>
<html lang="en">
<title>Switch statment</title>
</head>
<body>
<body>
<script language="javascript" type="text/javascript" >
    var a = parseInt(window.prompt("Enter a number"));
    var b= parseInt(prompt("Enter a number"));
    var c=0;
    var ch= prompt("Enter your choice");
    if(confirm("Would you like to Perform"))
      {
          switch(ch)
          { //case constant can be string also
             case "add" : c=a+b;
             alert("Result" +c);
             break;
```

```
            case "sub" : c=a-b;
            alert("Result" +c);
            break;
            case "mul" : c=a*b;
            alert("Result" +c);
            break;
            case "div" : c=a/b;
            alert("Result" +c);
            break;
            case "rem" : c=a%b;
            alert("Result" +c);
            break;
            default: alert("Invalid operation");
          }
      }
    else
          alert("Invalid Data");
</script>
</body>
</html>
</body>
</html>
```

<!-- finding the grade using switch -->

```
<html>
<head>
<title> switch </title>
</head>
<script language="javascript" type="text/javascript">
    var n1 = parseInt(window.prompt("Enter the marks in Sub1"));
    var n2 = parseInt(window.prompt("Enter the marks in Sub2"));
    var n3 = parseInt(window.prompt("Enter the marks in Sub3"));
    var avg= (n1+n2+n3)/3;
    var ch = parseInt(avg/10); //parse to int
```

```
    switch(ch)
     {
            case 10:
            case 9:
            case 8:
            case 7: window.alert("Distinction");
            break;
            case 6: window.alert("First Class");
            break;
            case 5: window.alert("Second Class");
            break;
            case 4: window.alert("Third Class ");
            break;
            default: window.alert("Fail ");
    }
</script>
<body>
</body>
</html>
//switch statement Is fall-through
//switch allows string constant as case option
```

<!-- Check a number is Amstrong or Not. -->

```
<html>
<head>
<title> while demo </title>
</head>
<script language="javascript" type="text/javascript">
    var n = parseInt(window.prompt("Enter a Number"));
    var r , sum=0;
    var m =n;
    while(n > 0)
```

```
      {
            r= n % 10;
            sum= sum+(r*r*r);
            n=parseInt(n/10); //here n/10 float-> convert to int
      }
            document.writeln("The sum is " +sum);

            if(sum == m)

                  alert("The num is Amstrong" +m);
            else
                  alert("The num is Not a Amstrong " +m);
</script>
<body>
</body>
</html>
```

<!-- finding the Reverse of a number -->

```
<html>
<head>
<title> do-while demo </title>
</head>
<script language="javascript" type="text/javascript">
    var n = parseInt(window.prompt("Enter a Number"));
    var r , sum=0;
    do
      {
            r= n % 10;
            sum= sum * 10 +r;
            n=parseInt(n/10); //here n/10 float-> convert to int
      }while(n!=0);
window.alert("The reverse num is " +sum);
</script>
<body>
</body>
```

```
</html>
```

```
<!-- Prime number or NOt-->
<html>
<head>
<title> for loop </title>
</head>
<script language="javascript" type="text/javascript">
var n = parseInt(window.prompt("Enter a Number"));
var flag=true;
for(var i=2 ; i <= parseInt(n/2); i++)
   {
     if (n % i == 0)
       {
            flag=false;
            break;
       }
   }
if(flag==true)
    window.alert("The number is Prime "+n);
else
    window.alert("The number is Not Prime "+n);
</script>
<body>
</body>
</html>
```

```
<!-- Multiplication Table -->
<html>
<head>
<title> for loop </title>

<script language="javascript" type="text/javascript">

    var n = parseInt(window.prompt("Enter a Number"));

    for(var i=1; i<=10 ; i++)

{
```

```
document.write(n*i); document.writeln("<BR>");
}
</script>
</head>
<body> Multiplication Table
</body>
</html>
```

<!-- function to find factorial -->

```
<html>
<head>
<title> Functions </title>
<script language="javascript" type="text/javascript">
    var n = parseInt(prompt("Enter a number"));
    var f = fact(n);
    document.writeln("The factorial is " +f);

    function fact( n )
     {
         var f =1;
         for(var i=1; i<=n ; i++) f= f*i;
         return f;
     }
</script>
</head>
<body>
</body>
</html>
```

<!-- Array initialization and creation -->

```
<html>
<head>
<title> Array Initialization and access </title>
<script language="javascript" type="text/javascript">
var data = new  Array(530  , "A.Ramesh "  , 9.8);
for(var i=0;i<data.length ; i++)
```

```
    document.writeln(data[i] + " ");
    document.writeln("<BR>");
var marks = new Array(87,81,77,88,76,92);
for(var i=0;i<marks.length ; i++)
    document.writeln(marks[i] + " ");
    document.writeln("<BR>");
var sum=0;

for (var x in marks) //for - in loop
    sum=sum+marks[x];
    document.writeln("The average is " + (sum/6));
</script>
</head>
<body>
</body>
</html>
```

<!-- Sorting array elements -->

```
<html>
<head>
<title> Array Initialization and access </title>
<script language="javascript" type="text/javascript">
    var n = parseInt(prompt("Enter the number of elements"));
    var a = new Array(n);
    window.alert("Enter the Array elements");
    for(var i=0 ; i < a.length ; i++)
          a[i] =parseInt(prompt("Enter the eement" +i));
    for(var i=0; i<a.length ; i++)
         {
          for(var j=i+1 ; j< a.length; j++)
             {
                if(a[i] > a[j])
                 {
                  var temp ; temp = a[i];
                  a[i] = a[j];
                  a[j] = temp;
                 }
```

```
            }
        }
     document.writeln("The elements after Sorting are <br>" );
    for(var i=0 ; i < a.length ; i++)
     document.writeln(a[i] + " "  );
</script>
</head>
<body>
</body>
</html>
```

<!-- Two dimensional arrays Addition-->

```
<html>
<head>
<script language="JavaScript">
var a = new Array(3);
    a[0] = new Array(3);
    a[1]= new Array(3);
    a[2] = new Array(3);
var b = new Array(3);
    b[0] = new Array(3);
    b[1]= new Array(3);
    b[2] = new Array(3);
var c = new Array(3);
    c[0] = new Array(3);
    c[1]= new Array(3);
    c[2] = new Array(3);
for(var i=0; i< a.length ; i++)
    for(var j=0; j<a[i].length ; j++)
     a[i][j] = parseInt(prompt("Enter the elements of A matrix"));
for(var i=0; i< b.length ; i++)
    for(var j=0; j<b[i].length ; j++)
     b[i][j] = parseInt(prompt("Enter the elements of B matrix"));
for(var i=0; i< c.length ; i++)
    for(var j=0; j<c[i].length ; j++)
     c[i][j] = a[i][j] + b[i][j]
```

```
for(var i=0; i< c.length ;  i++)
{

    for(var j=0; j<c[i].length ; j++)

      document.writeln(c[i][j] +"   ");

      document.writeln("<BR>" );
}
</script>
<head>
<body>
</body>
</html>
```

References and suggested readings

1. Javascript: This book includes: Javascript Basics For Beginners + Javascript Front End Programming + Javascript Back End Programming: 4 Paperback – 24 May 202 by Andy Vickler (Author)
2. HTML 5 Black Book, Covers CSS 3, JavaScript, XML, XHTML, AJAX, PHP and jQuery, 2ed by DT Editorial Services
3. The Little Book on CoffeeScript: The JavaScript Developer's Guide to Building Better Web Apps Paperback – Import, 21 February 2012 by Alex Maccaw (Author)
4. JavaScript: JavaScript Programming Made Easy for Beginners & Intermediates (Step By Step With Hands On Projects) Paperback – 12 September 2019 by Berg Craig (Author)
5. JSFiddle - Code Playground
6. JavaScript Examples | Programiz
7. JavaScript Exercises, Practice, Solution - w3resource

Dynamic QR CODE for further reading

4 Advance scripting

UNIT SPECIFICS

Through this unit we will discuss the following aspects:

- *JavaScript and objects DOM and web browser environments.*
- Forms and validations in DHTML, AJAX it's advantages & disadvantages.
- *XML It's usage DTD and Schema.*
- *XSLT and It's Applications comparison with XML.*
- *Introductory concepts of web Services.*

RATIONALE

This unit focuses on the Java Script Objects both predefined and user defined objects. Discussed DOM and various browser environments, like how to implement CSS, events, and controllers such as buttons to make web page as Dynamic by embedding same to HTML. It covers AJAX and it's advantages and disadvantages, implementation of web applications using AJAX.it also discuss the XML and it's usage and DTD, SCHEMA and XSLT and comparison of XML and XSLT and Introductory concepts of Web Servers.

PRE-REQUISITES

Problem Solving Skills

Object Oriented Programming

UNIT OUTCOMES

List of outcomes of this unit is as follows:

U4-O1: Explain Java Script Objects related to web Browsers

U4-O2: Describe the AJAX and it's role to design the Web Application

U4-O3: *Explain the XML, DTD ,Schema implementation and it's use .*

U4-O4: *Explain the XSLT and comparative study of XML and XSLT.*

U4-O5: *Describe the components of web services.*

Unit-4 Outcomes	EXPECTED MAPPING WITH COURSE OUTCOMES (1- Weak Correlation; 2- Medium correlation; 3- Strong Correlation)				
	CO-1	CO-2	CO-3	CO-4	CO-5
U4-O1	2	2	3	1	1
U4-O2	2	2	3	1	1
U4-O3	2	2	3	2	1
U4-O4	2	2	3	2	2
U4-O5	2	2	2	2	3

4. JavaScript Objects

JavaScript is an object –based scripting language.

- An object is a programmable entity used in script. JavaScript defines several built-in objects to use in different parts of the web page.
  Ex: Array, String Window, document etc.
- Every object has properties and methods.
- Property - is an attribute of a object.
  Ex: For Array object length is the property.
- Method – action or task that can be performed on the object.
  Ex: sort () is performed on Array object.
- Every HTML element in JavaScript is an Object.

- The commonly used Language objects are
  I. Array
  II. String

III. Math
IV. Number
V. Boolean
VI. Date

4.1. Array Object

- Array object allows creating and manipulating a series of values that are represented by a single name.
- The array can be constructed using
  - **Using array literal.**
    var data = [530 , "A.Ramesh" , 8.9];
  - **Creating instance of Array object**
    var data= new Array();
    data[0]= 530;
    data[1] = "A.Ramesh";
    data[2] = 8.9
  - **Using Constructor.**
    Var data = new Array(530 , "A.Ramesh" ,8.9);

4.1.1. The properties of Array object are

- **length**: returns the number of elements in the array.

4.1.2. The methods of Array Object are

Method Name	Description	Example

concat()	It gives back a fresh array object with one or more combined arrays.
	array.concat(arr1,arr2,. ,arrn)
		var a1=[20,30,40]; var a2=[60,70,80];
		var result=a1.concat(a2);
		document.writeln(result);

join()	It creates a new string by stringifying every element of an array. To separate the members of the specified array, any sort of separator can be used.
	array.join(separator)
		var a=[530 , "A.Ramesh" , 8.9] var result=arr.join()
		document.write(result);
		// var result=arr.join('-')

reverse()	It reverses the elements in the specified array.
	array.reverse()
		var a=["HYD","DELHI","CHENNAI"];
		var rev=a.reverse();
		document.writeln(rev);

sort()	It gives back the element of the array in the sorted order.
	array.sort()
		var a=[12,14,11,18,5];
		var result=arr.sort();
		document.writeln(result);

indexOf()	It looks up the provided element in the array and returns the first match's index.
	array.indexOf(element,index)
	
	element - It serves as the searchable element.
	
	index - It represents the position in the index at which a search begins. It is optional.
		var a=[12,32,22,31,32,58,28];
		var result= a.indexOf(32);
		document.writeln(result); //1
		
		Or
		var a=[32,22,31,32,58,28];
		var result= a.indexOf(32,2);
		document.writeln(result); //4

lastIndexOf()	It looks up the provided element in the array and returns the most recent match's index.
	array.lastIndexOf(element,index)
	
	element - This word refers to the element being searched for.
	
	index – It represents the starting index position for a search.
	It is optional.
		var a=[12,32,22,31,32,58,28];
		var result= a.lastIndexOf(32);
		document.writeln(result);
		
		Or
		var a=[32,22,31,32,58,28];
		var result= a.lastIndexOf (32,2);
		document.writeln(result);

push()	It adds one or more elements to the end of an array.
	array.push(element1,element2 elementn)
		var a=["HYD","CHENNAI"];
		a.push("DELHI");
		document.writeln(a);

pop()	It takes the last element of an array and then returns it.
	array.pop()
		var a=[20,34,56,78];
		document.writeln(a.pop());
		document.writeln(a);

slice()	It provides a new array that contains a replica of the specified portion.
	array. array.slice(start,end)
		var a=[12,13,48,28,56,88,34]
		var result=a.slice(2,4);
		document.writeln(result);

shift()	It removes the first element of an array and then returns it.
	array. shift()
		var a=[12,13,48,28,56,88,34]
		var result=a.shift();
		document.writeln(result);

unshift()	It introduces one or more elements at the start of the specified array.
	array. unshift(elem1,elem2,. ,elemn)
		var a=[12,13,48,28,56,88,34]
		var result=a.unshift(89,99);
		document.writeln(result);

4.2. String Object

- String object allows creating and manipulating a string of characters that are enclosed in single or double quotes.
- • A string in JavaScript is an object that depicts a group of characters. The strings are created in two ways.
  - **Using string literal.**
    var stringname="string value"
    var str="Welcome to JavaScript"; document.write(str);
  - **Using string object (Constructor)**
    var stname=new String("string literal");
    var str=new String ("Welcome to JavaScript");
    document.write(stringname);

4.2.1. The properties of String object are

- **length**: returns the number of characters in the string.

4.2.2. The methods of String Object are

Method Name	Description	Example
charAt()	It provides the char value present at the specified index. string.charAt(index)	var str="JavaScript"; document.writeln(str.charAt(4));
concat()	The combination of two or more strings is offered. string.concat(str1,str2,...,strn)	var x="welcome"; var y="to"; var z=" India"; document.writeln(x.concat(y,z));
indexOf()	It returns the char value given with the method's index position. indexOf(ch)	var x="JavaScript"; document.write(x.indexOf('a'));

	It begins by scanning the element using the provided index value before returning the specified char value's index location. indexOf(ch,index)	var str="welcome javascript"; document.write(str.indexOf('e',3));
	It gives the first character in the string that was supplied to the method's index position. indexOf(str);	var str=" webtech is to do web "; document.write(str.indexOf("web"));
	It begins by looking for the element using the specified index value before returning the index position of the string's first character. indexOf(str,index);	var str=" webtech is to do web "; document.write(str.indexOf("web",2));
match()	It finds a defined regular expression in a supplied string and returns that regular expression if a match appears. string.match(regexp)	var str="Javascript"; document.writeln(str.match("Java"));

replace()	It substitutes the supplied replacement for the given string.
	string.replace(originalstr,newstr)
		var str="secbad";
		document.writeln(str.replace("sec","hyd"));
		var str="secbad is famous for irani chai , secbad has clock tower";
		document.writeln(str.replace(/sec/g,"hyd"));

search()	If a match is found, it looks for a specific regular expression in a supplied string and provides its position.
	string.search(regexp)
		var str="JavaScript is a scripting lan guage. Scripting languages are often interpreted";
		document.writeln(str.search("scripti ng"));
		document.writeln(str.search(/Script ing/));
		document.writeln(str.search(/Script ing/i));
		// i- ignore case sensitive

substring()	It is utilised to retrieve the specific portion of the given string based on the defined index.
	string.substring(start,end) ;
		var str="hyderabad";
		document.writeln(str.substring(2,4));
		var str="hyderabad ";
		document.writeln(str.substring(3));

toLowerCase()	The specified string is changed to lowercase letters. string.toLowerCase()	var str = "weCOME to HYD"; document.writeln(str.toLowerCase());
toUpperCase()	The specified string is changed to uppercase letters. string.toUpperCase()	var str = " weCOME to HYD "; document.writeln(str.toUpperCase());
lastIndexOf()	It gives back the last place of the char value that was supplied to the method. lastIndexOf(ch)	var web="Learn JavaScript on Javas cript"; document.write(web.lastIndexOf('a'));
	It begins scanning the element from the given index value in inverse order and then returns the supplied char value's index position. lastIndexOf(ch,index)	var web="Learn JavaScript on Javasript" ; document.write(web.lastIndexOf('a',10));

	It returns the first character in the string that was supplied to the method at position index. lastIndexOf(str)	var web="Learn JavaScript on Javasript "; document.write(web.lastIndexOf("Java"));
	It begins looking up the element using the specified index value and then displays the index location of the string's first character. lastIndexOf(str,index)	var web="Learn JavaScript on Javasript "; document.write(web.lastIndexOf("Java",19));
substr()	It is used to retrieve a portion of the given string based on the starting position and length that are specified. string.substr(start,length)	var str="hyderabad"; document.writeln(str.substr(3,4)); var str="hyderabad"; document.writeln(str.substr(4));

slice()	It is used to retrieve the specified portion of the string. We can assign both positive and negative indexes.
	string.slice(start,end)
		var str = "Javascript";
		document.writeln(str.slice(2,5));
		var str = "Javascript";
		document.writeln(str.slice(5));
		//from begining
		document.writeln(str.slice(-5));
		//end of string

toString()	It offers a string that represents the specific object. object.toString()	var str=new String("Javascript") document.writeln(str.toString());
valueOf()	It offers the basic string object value. string.valueOf()	var str=new String("Javascript"); document.writeln(str.valueOf());

4.3. Date Object

- Date object allows to create and manipulate date and time.
- The JavaScript date object can be used to get year, month and day.
- We can display a timer on the webpage with the help of JavaScript date object.
- Using different Date constructors to create date objects. It provides methods to get and set day, month, year, hour, minute and seconds.
- The constructors of Date object are
    - Date()
      var d = new Date( );
      Date(milliseconds)
      var d1 = new Date(1542568925); // 01 January 1970 plus + msec
    - Date(dateString)
      var d2 = new Date("2015-03-25"); var d = new Date("03/25/2015");
      var d3 = new Date("Mar 25 2015");
      var d4 = new Date("January 25 2015");
      var d5 = new Date("October 13, 2014 11:13:00");
    - Date(year, month, day, hours, minutes, seconds, milliseconds)
      var d6 = new Date(2018, 11, 24, 10, 33, 30, 0);
      var d7 = new Date(2018, 11, 24, 10, 33, 30);
      var d8= new Date(2018, 11, 24, 10, 33); var d = new Date(2018, 11, 24);
      var d9= new Date(2018);

4.3.1. The methods of Date Object are

Method Name	Description	Example

getDate()	It gives back an integer value between 1 and 31 that, based on local time, reflects the day for the supplied date.
	
	dateObj.getDate()
		var d=new Date();
		document.writeln("Today's day: "+d.getDate()
		);
		var d=new Date("July 8, 2019 16:22:10");
		document.writeln(d.getDate())

getDay()	It returns the integer value between 0 and 6 that represents the day of the week on the basis of local time.
	
	dateObj.getDay()
		var day=new Date();
		document.writeln(day.getDay());
		var day=new Date("July 8, 2019 16:22:10");
		document.writeln(day.getDay())

getMonth()	It gives back an integer value between 0 and 11 that, based on local time, reflects the month.
	
	dateObj.getMonth()
		var date=new Date();
		document.writeln(date.getMonth()+1);
		var date=new Date("July 8, 2019 16:22:10");
		document.writeln(date.getMonth()+1)

getFullYear()	It gives back an integer value based on local time that reflects the year.
	
	dateObj.getFullYear()
		var year=new Date();
		document.writeln(year.getFullYear());
		var year=new Date("July 8, 2019 16:22:10”);
		document.writeln(year.getFullYear());

getHours()	It provides a return value that is an integer between 0 and 23 that represents the hours based on local time.
	
	dateObj.getHours()
		var hour=new Date();
		document.writeln(hour.getHours());
		var hour=new Date("July 8, 2019 16:22:10");
		document.writeln(hour.getHours());

getMinutes()	It returns an integer value between 0 and 59 that, when based on local time, indicates the minutes.
	
	dateObj.getMinutes()
		var min=new Date();
		document.writeln(min.getMinutes());
		var min=new Date("July 8, 2019 16:22:10");
		document.writeln(min.getMinutes());

getSeconds()	It returns an integer value between 0 and 59 that, when based on local time, reflects the number of seconds.
	// from 01 January 1970
	
	dateObj.getSeconds()
		var sec=new Date();
		document.writeln(sec.getSeconds());
		var sec=new Date("July 8, 2019 16:22:10");
		document.writeln(sec.getSeconds());

getMilliseconds()	It returns the milliseconds based on local time as an integer value between 0 and 999.
	
	dateObj.getMilliseconds()
		var milli =new Date();
		document.writeln(milli.getMilliseconds());
		var milli =new Date("July 8, 2019 16:22:10");
		document.writeln(milli.getMilliseconds());

setDate()	It returns the milliseconds based on local time as an integer value between 0 and 999.(1 to 31) setDate(dd);	var d = new Date(); d.setDate(15);

setDay()	It establishes the specific day of the week based on local time. (0 to 6) setDay(day)	var d = new Date(); d.setDay(3);

setFullYear()	Using local time, it establishes the year value for the supplied date.
	
	setFullYear(yyyy,mm,dd);
		var d = new Date(); d.setFullYear(2020);
		var d = new Date();
		d.setFullYear(2020, 11, 3);

setMonth()	On the basis of local time, it establishes the month value for the supplied date.(0-11) setMonth(mm)	var d = new Date(); d.setMonth(11);
setHours()	Using local time, it establishes the hour value for the supplied date. setHours(hh , mm , ss);	var d = new Date(); d.setHours(22);
setMinutes()	On the basis of local time, it establishes the minute value for the chosen date. setMinutes(mm,ss)	var d = new Date(); d.setMinutes(30);
setSeconds()	On the basis of local time, it sets the second value for the provided date. setSeconds(ss)	var d = new Date(); d.setSeconds(30);

serMillisecon ds()	On the basis of local time, it determines the millisecond value for the provided date. setMilliSeconds(msec); // 01 January 1970	var d = new Date(); d.setMilliSeconds(12563254825);
toString()	It gives back the date as a string.	Var d = new Date(); var str = d.toString();
valueOf()	It provides the Date object's basic value.	var d = new Date(); var str = d.valueOf();
Similarly all the methods with UTC time zone.(Coordinated Universal Time (UTC)) *Eg: setUTCDate() , getUTCMonth() etc*		

4.4. Math Object

- The JavaScript Math object provides several constants and methods to perform mathematical operation.
- The Math object doesn't have constructors.

4.4.1. The methods of Date Object are

Method Name	Description	Example

abs()	It returns the absolute value of the given number.
	
	Math.abs(num)
		document.writeln(Math.abs(-4));
		document.writeln(Math.abs(-7.8));
		document.writeln(Math.abs('-4'));
		document.writeln(Math.abs(null)); //0
		document.writeln(Math.abs("string"));
		//NaN

sign()	It gives back the supplied number's sign.
	
	Math.sign(num)
		document.writeln(Math.sign(12)); //1
		document.writeln(Math.sign(-12)) ; //-1
		document.writeln(Math.sign(0));//0

sqrt()	It returns the square root of the given number.
	Math.sqrt(num)
		document.writeln(Math.sqrt(16));
		document.writeln(Math.sqrt(12));
		document.writeln(Math.sqrt(-9));//NaN

cbrt()	It provides the provided number's cube root. Math.cbrt(num)	document.writeln(Math.cbrt(8)); document.writeln(Math.cbrt(-64));

ceil()	It provides the least integer result that is larger than or equal to the inputted value.
	
	Math.ceil(num)
		document.writeln(Math.ceil(7.2)); //8
		document.writeln(Math.ceil(0.2)); //1
		document.writeln(Math.ceil(-7.2));//-7
		document.writeln(Math.ceil(-0.2)); //0

floor()	The greatest integer value that is lower than or equal to the supplied number is returned..
	
	Math.floor(num)
		document.writeln(Math.floor(7.2)); //7
		document.writeln(Math.floor(0.2)); //0
		document.writeln(Math.floor(-7.2));//-8
		document.writeln(Math.floor(-0.2)); //- 1

round()	It returns the provided number's closest integer value.
	
	Math.round(num)
		document.writeln(Math.round(7.2)); //7
		document.writeln(Math.round(0.6)); //1
		document.writeln(Math.round(-7.2));
		//-7
		document.writeln(Math.round(-0.6));
		//-1

trunc()	It gives back an integer portion of the inputted number.
	
	Math.trunc(num)
		document.writeln(Math.trunc(12.24));
		//12 document.writeln(Math.trunc(0.84));
		//0
		document.writeln(Math.trunc(-12.24));
		//-12
		document.writeln(Math.trunc(-0.84));
		//0

max()	It returns the given numbers' highest value. Math.max(num1,num2,. ,numN)	document.writeln(Math.max(22,34,12)); //34 document.writeln(Math.max(-10,-24,-12)); // -10
min()	It returns the given numbers' minimal value. Math.min(num1,num2,...,numN)	document.writeln(Math.min(22,34,12)); //12 document.writeln(Math.min(-10,-24,-12)); // -24

pow()	It gives back base value raised to the power of the exponent.
	
	Math.pow(base,exponent)
		document.writeln(Math.pow(2,3));
		document.writeln(Math.pow(5,2.4));
		document.writeln(Math.pow(2,-3));

random()	It provides a random number between 0 (inclusive) and 1 (exclusive). Math.random()	document.writeln(Math.random())
sin()	It provides the number's sine as a response. Math.sin(num)	document.writeln(Math.sin(1));
cos()	It gives back the given number's cosine. Math.cos(num)	document.writeln(Math.cos(1));
tan()	It provides the provided number's tangent back. Math.tan(num)	document.writeln(Math.tan(1));
sinh()	It provides the provided number's hyperbolic sine. Math.sinh(num)	document.writeln(Math.sinh(-1)); document.writeln(Math.sinh(0));

cosh()	It provides the provided number's hyperbolic cosine. Math.cosh(num)	document.writeln(Math.cosh(-1)); document.writeln(Math.cosh(0));
tanh()	It gives the provided number's hyperbolic tangent. Math.tanh(num)	document.writeln(Math.tanh(-1)

4.4.2. The Math object constants /Properties

Property Name	Description	Example
LN2	Natural logarithm of 2, approximately 0.693.	var x= Math.LN2
LN10	Natural logarithm of 10, approximately 2.302.	. var x=Math.LN10
LOG2E	Base 2 logarithm of E, approximately 1.442.	. var x=Math.LOG2E
LOG10E	Base 10 logarithm of E, approximately 0.434.	var x=Math.LOG10E
PI	Ratio of the circumference of a circle to its diameter, approximately 3.14159.	var x=Math.PI
SQRT1_2	Square root of 1/2; equivalently, 1 over the square root of 2, approximately 0.707.	var x=Math.SQRT1_2
SQRT2	Square root of 2, approximately 1.414.	var x=Math.SQRT2

4.5. Number Object

- The JavaScript number object enables you to represent a numeric value. It may be integer or floating-point.
- JavaScript number object follows IEEE standard to represent the floating-point numbers.
- The constructors for Number Object is
    - Number() Number(value)
      Eg: var n=new Number(16);

4.5.1. The Number object constants /Properties

MIN_VALUE	returns the largest minimum value.
MAX_VALUE	returns the largest maximum value.
POSITIVE_INFINITY	returns positive infinity, overflow value.
NEGATIVE_INFINITY	returns negative infinity, overflow value.
NaN	represents "Not a Number" value.

4.5.2. The Number object methods are

Method Name	Description	Example

isFinite()	The value's finiteness is determined.
	
	Number.isFinite(num)
		var x=0;
		var y=11;
		var z=-111;
		document.writeln(Number.isFinite(x));
		//true
		document.writeln(Number.isFinite(y));
		//true
		document.writeln(Number.isFinite(z));
		//true

isInteger()	It determines if the supplied value is an integer.
	
	Number.isInteger(num)
		var y=1;
		document.writeln(Number.isInteger(y));
		//true

parseInt()	The given string is changed into an integer number.
	Number.parseInt(string, radix)
	document.writeln(Number.parseInt(a, 10));
	//decimal value
	
	document.writeln(Number.parseInt(a,
		var a="50";
		var d="50String";
		var b="welcome2019";
		document.writeln(Number.parseInt(a));
		//50
		document.writeln(Number.parseInt(d));
		//50

	8));
	//octal value
	
	document.writeln(Number.parseInt(a, 16));
	//hexa decimal value
		document.writeln(Number.parseInt(b));
		//NaN

parseFloat()	It creates a floating point number from the provided string.
	Number.parseFloat(string)
		var b="50.25"
		var d="50.25String"
		document.writeln(Number.parseInt(b));
		document.writeln(Number.parseInt(d));

toString()	It returns the given number in the form of string. toString()	var n=new Number(16); document.writeln(n.toString());
valueOf()	valueOf()	document.writeln(n.valueOf());
toExponential ()	It gives back a string that reflects the provided number in exponential notation. Number. toExponential(num)	var a=989721; document.writeln(a.toExponential()); 9.89721e+5

4.6. Boolean Object

- The Boolean object represents two values, either "true" or "false".
- If value parameter is omitted or is 0, -0, null, false, NaN, undefined, or the empty string (""), the object has an initial value of false.

```
var val= new Boolean(value);
var x = Boolean(10>9) ; // true
var val= new Boolean(true); //true
var val= new Boolean(0); //false
var x= false;
var y= new Boolean(false); // (x == y) is true because x and y have equal
values
var x = false;
```

var y = new Boolean(false); // (x == y) is false because x and y have different types

4.6.1. The Boolean object methods are

Method Name	Description	Example
toString()	Depending on the object's value, this function returns a string that is either "true" or "false". boolean.toString()	var flag = new Boolean(false); document.write ("flag.toString is : " + flag.toString());
valueOf()	Returns the primitive value of the specified Boolean object. boolean.valueOf()	. var flag = new Boolean(false); document.write("flag valueOf is : " + flag.valueOf());

4.7. Window Object

- window represents the web browser open window.
- If webpage is divided into frames, each frame corresponds to a separate window object.

4.7.1. The properties of the window object are

Property Name	Description
closed	determines whether a window has been closed by returning a Boolean value.
default Status	restores or sets the window's status bar's default text
document	gives the window's Document object back.
history	Returns the History object for the window
location	Returns the Location object for the window
name	Sets or returns the name of a window

navigator	Returns the Navigator object for the window
outerHeight	Returns the height of the browser window, including toolbars/scrollbars
outerWidth	Returns the width of the browser window, including toolbars/scrollbars
status	sets or retrieves the text in a window's status bar.

4.7.2. The methods of window Object are

Method Name	Description	Example
alert()	Shows an alert box with a message and an OK button. alert(message)	alert("Hello Welcome to Javascript");
confirm()	Displays a dialog box with a message and an OK and a Cancel button. A confirm box is often used if you want the user to verify or accept something. confirm(message)	confirm("Perform or not?");
prompt()	Displays a dialog box that prompts the visitor for input. prompt(text, defaultText)	prompt("enter a no", "12")
blur()	Removes focus from the current window. window.blur()	myWindow.blur();
focus()	Changes focus to the selected window. window.focus()	myWindow.focus();
close()	Closes the current window. window.close()	myWindow.close();

open()	Opens a new browser window.
	window.open(URL, name, specs, replace);
	
	URL- Optional, any URL.
	name – Optional , the value can be _blank,_top,_parent,_self, name of window.
	Specs - can be fullscreen=yes|no|1|0, height=pixels, status=yes|no|1|0, scrollbars= yes|no|1|0, resizable= yes|no|1|0, titlebar=yes|no|1|0, toolbar=yes|no|1|0, top=pixels, width=pixels.
	Replace – can be
	true - URL replaces the current document in the history list.
	false - URL creates a new entry in the history list
		window.open("https://www.google.com");
		
		var myWindow = window.open("", "MsgWindow", "width=200,height=100");
		
		var myWindow = window.open("", "_self");
		
		window.open("https://www.google.com", "_blank", "toolbar=yes,scrollbars=yes,resizable=yes,top=500,left=500,width=400,height=400");

moveTo()	repositions a window to the desired location. window.moveTo(x, y)	myWindow.moveTo(500, 100);
print()	Prints the content of the current window. window.print(). //a default printer is assigned to get current page print.	window.print()

4.8. Document Object

- Document Object represents the HTML document or webpage that is currently opened in the web browser.
- • A document object is created when an HTML document is loaded into a web browser.

4.8.1. The properties of document object are

Property Name	Description
activeElement	returns the document's currently focused element.
anchors	returns a collection of all< a> elements in the document with a name attribute.
applets	Returns a collection of all the <applet> elements in the document
body	Sets or returns the document's body (the <body> element)
close	Closes the output stream previously opened with document.open()
cookie	Returns all name/value pairs of cookies in the document
doctype	returns the document's related Document Type Declaration.
documentElement	Brings back the Document Element of the document (the <html> element)
title	returns or sets the document's title
URL	Returns the full URL of the HTML document
lastModified	Returns the date and time the document was last modified

4.8.2. The methods of document Object are

Method Name	Description		Example
getElementById()	Returns the element that has the ID attribute with the specified value. document.getElementById(elemen tID) elementID : The ID attribute's value of the element you want to get		document.getElementById("101");
getElementsByNam e()	Brings back a NodeList containing all elements with a specified name. document.getElementsByName(n ame)		var x = document.getElementsByName("fname");

getElements ByTagName()	Brings back a NodeList containing all elements with the specified tag name. document.getElementsByTagNam e(tagname)		var x = document.getElementsByTagName("LI");
getElements ByClass Name()	Returns a NodeList containing all elements with the specified class name. document.getElementsByClassName(classname)		var x = document.getElementsByClassName("example");
write()	Writes HTML expressions or JavaScript code to a document. document.write(exp1, exp2, exp3, ...)		document.write("Hello World!");
writeln()	The same as write(), but after each statement, a newline character is added. document.writeln(exp1, exp2, exp3, ...)		document.writeln("Hello World!");

4.9. History Object

- Represents a list of URLs that the user has already accessed.
- If the webpage uses frames, each frame separately has its own history object i.e. each has its own list of URLs.

4.9.1. The properties of the history object are

Property Name	Description
length	gives the number of URLs in the history list.

4.9.2. The methods of history Object are

Method Name	Description	Example

back()	carries out a history list load for the preceding URL.
	history.back()
		function goBack()
		{
		window.history.back();
		}

forward()	Loads the next URL in the history list.
	history.forward()
		function goForward() {
		window.history.forward();
		}

go()	Loads a specific URL from the history list. history.go(number|URL)
	back -> -ve
	forward-> _ve
		function goBack() {
		window.history.go(-2);
		}

4.10. Navigator Object

- Allows to access various information about user's web browser.

4.10.1. The properties of navigator object are

Property Name	Description
appCodeName	Returns the code name of the browser.
appName	Returns the name of the browser
appVersion	Returns the version information of the browser
cookieEnabled	Determines whether cookies are enabled in the browser
platform	Returns for which platform the browser is compiled
language	Returns the language of the browser
product	Returns the engine name of the browser

4.10.2. The methods of the Navigator Object are

Method Name	Description	Example
javaEnabled()	Indicates whether Java is enabled in the browser. navigator.javaEnabled()	var x = "Java Enabled: " + navigator.javaEnabled();

4.11. Location Object

- Allows to access information about the URL of the webpage that is currently opened in a window or frame.

4.11.1. The properties of location object are

Property Name	Description
host	a URL's hostname and port number are set or returned.
hostname	retrieves or sets a URL's hostname
href	returns or sets the whole URL
pathname	sets or gets the URL's path name
port	sets or receives a URL's port number
protocol	establishes or returns a URL's protocol
search	returns or sets the URL's "query string"

4.11.2. The methods of location Object are

Method Name	Description	Example
assign()	Loads a new document. location.assign(URL)	location.assign("https://www.gmail.com");
reload()	Reloads the current document location.reload(flag) flag can be false - Default. Reloads the current page from the cache.	location.reload();

	true - Reloads the current page from the server	
replace()	Replaces the current document with a new one. location.replace(newURL)	location.replace("https://www.google.com");

4.12. screen Object

- Allows to access different information about the user's screen

4.12.1. The properties of screen object are

Property Name	Description
availHeight	Returns the height of the screen (excluding the Windows Taskbar)
availWidth	Returns the width of the screen (excluding the Windows Taskbar)
colorDepth	Returns the bit depth of the color palette for displaying images
height	Returns the total height of the screen
width	Returns the total width of the screen
pixelDepth	Returns the color resolution (in bits per pixel) of the screen

4.13. Frames

- HTML frames are used to divide the web browser window into multiple sections, where each section can be loaded separately with a web page.
- Frames allow you to view multiple pages on the same window at a time.
- The element <u><frameset></u> is used to hold the collection of frames. This element configures the frames on window/browsers.
- A frameset is a collection of frames.
- <u><Frame></u> tag is used to create frames.
- <Frameset> element actually takes the place of <body> element in a document that displays frames
- <Frameset> allows to organise both vertical & horizontal frames, or both.

4.13.1. <FRAMESET> Tag

- It structures a document using frames.
- Uses <frame> element.

The attributes are:-

- **border–** to adjust the border thickness for each frame in the frameset (0 to n)
- **bordercolor–** sets the border colour for every frame in the fameset.
- **cols–** determines the number of columns in the frameset (screen area as a percentage). Eg: 25%
- → To show remaining space)
- **frameborder—** Whether the border is set to frames (or) not. (yes or no)
- **framespacing—** Sets pixel spacing between frames
- **rows–** Sets the no.of rows (frames) in the frameset.(% age or *).
- **style–** Inline style indicating how to render the element.
- **title–** Holds additional information for the element. (inline tooltips).

4.13.2. <Frame> tag

- Used to create frames

The attributes are:-

- **bordercolor—** Sets the colour used for frame border
- **datafld—** Name of the data source object's column that bound data
- **datasrc—** reveals the URL or ID of the item serving as the data source for the element.
- **frameborder–** determines whether the frame is surrounded by boundaries.
- **marginheight–** Sets the size of top and bottom margins used in frame. (in pixels)
- **marginwidth–** Sets the size of right and left margins used in the frame (in pixels)
- **name–** Sets name of the frame

- **scrolling–** Determines scrollbar action. (auto, yes ,no).
- **src–** Specifiers the url of the frame document.
- **style–** a rendering instruction inline style for the element.
- **title–** include more data (tool tips).

Ex: 1. Creating Vertical Frames.

```
(i) <frameset  cols = "25%, 75%">
      -------
      -------             // frames — 2
    </frameset>

(ii) <frameset cols = "25%, *">
      -------
      -------             //frames — 2
    </frameset>

(iii) <frameset  cols = "25%, 62%, *">
      -------
      -------             // 3 frames
```

Ex. 2. Creating horizontal frames.

```
(i) <frameset rows = "30%, 70%">
      -------
      -------             // 2 frames
    </frameset>

(ii) <frameset rows = "30%, 52%, *">
      -------
      -------
    </frameset>
```

4.14. Sample Programmes

4.14.1. Program to Create Vertical frames

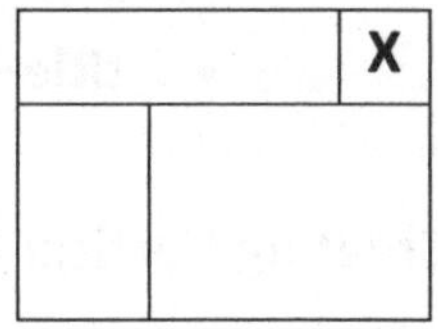


```
<html>
 <frameset cols = “ 25% ,*” bordercolor = “red”>
 <frame name = “f1” src = “index.html”>
 <frame name = “f2” src = “content.html”>
 </frameset>
  </html>
```

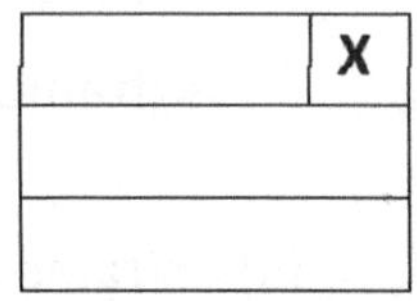

4.14.2. Program to Create the horizontal frames

```
<frameset rols = “27%, *”>
 <frame name = “f1” src = “index.html”>
  <frame name = “f2” src = “content.html”>
   </frameset>
```

4.14.3. Program to create the nested frames

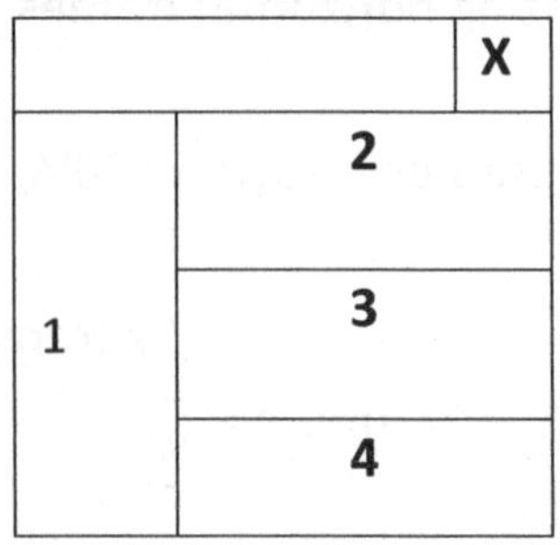


```
    <frameset cols = “25%, 75%” >
     <frame src = “index.html”  name = “f1” >
     <frameset  rows = “20%, 71%, *”>
        <frame name = “f2”  src = “head.html”>
         <frame  name = “f3” src =
“content.html”>
          <frame  name = “f4” src = “copy.html”>
      </frameset>
      </frameset>
```

4.14.4. Creating vertical frames using Pixels

```
<frameset cols = "200, *'>
  <frame name = "f1" src ="head.html" >
    <frame name = "f2" src ="content.html" >
</frameset>
```

4.14.5. Program to create nested frames.

```
<html>
 <head>
       <title>named frames </title>
  </head>
   <body >
       <frameset cols = "30% , *">
        <frame name = "f1" src = "index.html" >
        <frame name = "f2" src = "content.html" >
       </frameset>
       </body>
       </html>
```

Index.html

```
<html>
 <body>
     <a href = "cse.html"  target = "f2">cse</a>
 <BR><a href = "ece.html" target = "f2">ece </a>
  </body>
   </html>
```

" if target = "new window" → displays the web page in a new window".

4.15. HTML Forms & HTML Controls

- Forms are used to handle the html controls like buttons, text fields, text area etc.
- HTML forms are used to submit the data to the server for processing, i.e.. A form packages all the data from a group of controls and all the data is sent to the server.
- Forms are not visible objects on the screen.
- The <FORM> tag is used to create forms
- A web page can have multiple forms also.

4.15.1. <Form> tag

- Creates a HTML form, used to enclose HTML controls like buttons, text fields etc.

i. **The attributes are**

- **accept –** List of content types that a server processing this from will handle correctly.
- **action –** Gives the URL that will handle form data in controls when the submit button is clicked.
- **autocomplete –** If it is set to "true", automatically depending on previous entries made by the user in controls like text fields.
- **class –** Class of the element
- **method –** Indicates a HTTP method or protocol for sending data to the target action URL (By default get). The values are get & post.
- **name –** Name to the form to reference in the script code
- **style –** Inline style indicating how to render the element.
- **target –** Indicates a named frame for the browser to display the form results in.
- **title –** Holds additional information (displayed in tooltip).

ii. **The various events on a form can be :-**

- onclick , onblus, ondray, onkeydown,
- onkeypress, onkeyup, onmousedown,

- onmouseenter, onmouseleave, onsubmit, onreset etc.

Ex:

```
<body>
        <form name = "form1" method ="post">

                :

                user controls

                :

        </form>
</body>
```

- • The goal of an HTML form is to enable user input and data transmission from one end to the other (client, server) via a web server.
- • The submit button on each form helps convey information to the Action URL by way of the server.

4.15.2. HTML Controls

- Users interact with forms using HTML controls.
- The fundamental components of a web page form are HTML Controls.
- HTML controls improve the usability of a web page.
- Users use HTML controls to input data into web page forms.
- HTML Controls are placed/created using <INPUT> tag.

iii. **<input> Tag**

- Used to add HTML Controls, for sending input data.
- The attributes are :-

Attribute	Value	Description
align	Left,right, top, text top, middle, absmiddle, baseline, bottom,absbottom	Alignment of text following the image.(used for image control).

alt	Any text	Alternate text for the image. Used only with image control.
type	Button, checkbox file, hidden image, password, radio, reset, submit text etc.	Type of the input element. The default value is "text".
checked	Checked	Input element is checked when loaded on a web server (used for radio & checked).
disabled	Disabled	while the web server loads, disables the input element. such that the user cannot choose or write on it.
maxlength	Number	Maximum no.of characters allowed in text field. (only with 'text').
name	Field name	Unique name for the element. Used with all controls.
readonly	Readonly	The value of this field cannot be modified (used with 'text').
src	URL	URL of the image to display. (used with 'image')
value	Any text	sets the caption

4.15.3. Adding a Button :–

- Used to create a button in the HTML form.
- The type value is "button", in <input> tag.
  <input type = "button" value = "clickhere">

Submit Here

iv. **Adding a Submit Button: –**

- When the submit button is clicked , The form's entire contents are submitted to the web server.
- When a user clicks, the information in the form is sent to the URL listed in the <form>.
- The type value is "submit" in <input> tag
  <input type = "submit " value = "Submit Here">

v. **The attributes for submit button are :-**

- **name** – Name of the button
- **value** – Text to be placed on button
- **align** – provides the alignment of button
- **tabindex** – When there are numerous buttons on a webpage, the tab order of the buttons is used.

Clear

4.15.4. Adding a Reset Button:-

- The reset button enables the user to erase all information input in text fields, restore the form to its default state, and begin anew.
- • The controls in the form revert to their initial state when the user clicks, and the values in the fields are cleared.
- Type value is "reset" in <input > tag
  <input type = "reset" value = "clear">

4.15.5. Adding text field :-

- Used to add a one line text in the form
- Type value is “text” in <input> tag

  <input type = “text” name = “ first name” value = “enter” size = 20/>

4.15.6. Adding a checkbox:-

- • The user can click on a little box that has a check mark in it to choose or clear it. Allows to select more options.

  CE : < input type = “checkbox” name = “branch” value = “CE” >
  CSE: <input type = “checkbox” name = “branch” value = “CSE” checked>

4.15.7. Adding a radio button:-

- When selected, it appears as a circle with a dot in the centre.
- Radio buttons work in mutually exclusive groups and only one radio button can be selected at a time.
- The type value is “radio ” in <input> tag

  Male: <input type = “radio” name =” gender” value = “yes”/>
  **
**
  Female : <input type = “radio” name = “gender” value = “no”/>

4.15.8. Adding a Text Area:-

- It has numerous lines of text input and displays the text that is entered there.

- No.of rows and columns are specified using rows & columns attribute.
- The element <Textarea> is used to create it.

  < textarea rows=’10’ cols=’30’ >
  Write text if required initially
  < /textarea >

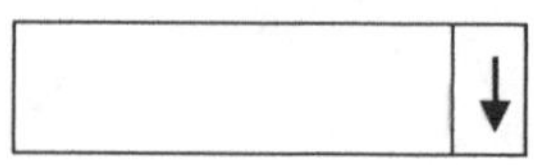

4.15.9. Adding a selection Control:--

- It is a drop down list used to select any of the options listed.
- <select > element is used to create it.
- < select > used < option > and < opt group > tags.
- < option > to specify the item of list.
- < opt group > allows to group choices in the form.

The Courses are :
< select >
< optgroup label = "UG courses" >
< option value = "cse" > CSE < /option >
< option value = "ECE" > ECE < /option >
< /optgroup >

< optgroup label = "PG courses" >
< option value = "MTech" > MTECH < /option >
< option value = "MBA"> MBA < /option >
< /optgroup >
< /select >

vi. **To select multiple options**

<select multiple> → (or) MULTIPLE

-------------</select>

4.15.10. Adding a file Control:-

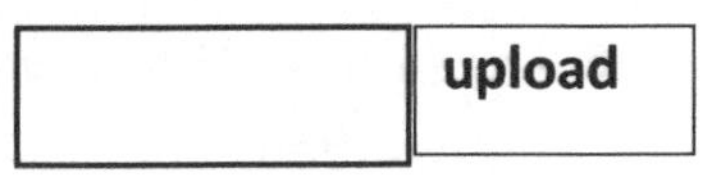

- Used to create a file input for the form.
- Used to Upload files.
- The type value is " file " in < input > tag.
  < input type = " file " name = " filename "
  Value = " " size = 30 >
- The file control has two controls a text field and a browse button.
- When browse button clicked, the user can select a file from the disk.

4.15.11. Adding a hidden control:-

- • It keeps concealed data, which viewers cannot see unless they view the page source.
- The type value is " hidden " in < input > tag.
  < input type = " hidden " name = " hi " Value = " welcome to forms " >

4.15.12. Adding an image control:-

- It is similar to submit button.
- when user click on image, the form data sent to webserver.
- The mouse coordinates are also passed to the form's action URL.
- The type value is " image " in < input tag >
  < input type = " image " src = " filepath " name = " submit " value = " SUBMIT " >

4.15.13. Adding password control:-

- Creates a password text field, it masks the typed input.
- The type value is " password " in < input > tag .
  < input type = " password " name = " pwd " size = 25 >

4.15.14. Adding Action control:-

• The <form> tag's action URL and method are used to direct the form data to the server.

- **action** – The server's physical address, or URL, is where the user data is forwarded.

When submit button clicked.

- **method** – The attribute has two values get & post.
  1. method = " get " —> indicates that the web browser must encrypt the form data **(by default)** into a URL.
  —> the form data visible in the address bar.
  —> used for small forms.

2. method = " post " —> indicates that the message body contains the form data.

—> the form data invisible (hide)

—> used for large size forms.

—> Send data as a packet.

```
< form action = " demo.html " method = " post "
            -----------------
            -----------------
< /form >
```

4.16. CASCADING STYLE SHEETS

- In comparison to the limited usage of tags and attributes, style sheets offer a mechanism to customise entire pages at once and in considerably greater detail.
- Style sheets provide tag and attribute based style to improve look feel of a webpage.
- Style sheets are implemented with the Cascading Style Sheets (CSS) specification.
- CSS is standardized by w3c, called CSS specifications.
- The CSS defines a rule with set of properties.

  Ex : H1 { font-size : 20 pt }

  Font-size —> property of css

  20 pt —> value of css property .
- Style sheets are just a list of rules.
- The style sheets implementation varies from browser to browser
- The Styles are created by three ways.
  1. Embedded style sheets (Internal style sheets)
  2. External style Sheets
  3. Inline style sheets

4.16.1. Inline Style Sheets

- The style attribute of every html tag is used to define the styles
- Used to apply styles for a particular portion or to a particular element

Ex: setting color of table cells

```
< table border=3 >
< TR >
   < th style = " background-color : #112233" > Name< /th >
   < th style = " background-color : #BBCCDD "> Place< /th >
< /TR >
< TR >
   < TD style = " color:green; font-style :italic " >
   1011< /TD >
   < TD style = " color:red; font-style :bold " >
   A.Ramesh< /TD >
   < TD style = " color:blue; font-style :italic " >
   Hyderabad< /TD >
< /TR >

< /table >
```

4.16.2. Embedded Styles / Internal Style sheets

- Using inline styles, if several parts of the page adhere to the same style, all styles must be specified repeatedly
- If same styles are repeated in multiple parts of the webpage Embedded Styles are used.
- Embedded style sheets are for a webpage.
- The styles applied throughout the webpage are collected and placed in one place
- Embedded styles are specified in < style > tag of < head > element.

Ex: < html >

```
< head >
< title > embedded styles < /title >
```

```
< style type " text/css " >
BODY { background : #AABBCC ; color : green }
A: link { color: red }
P { font-style : italic }
< /style>
```

For tag

For particular attribute

```
< /head >
< body >
Welcome to Hyderabad
< a href= " demo. html " > click here < /a >
< p > India is rich in producing ... < / p >
<body >
< /html >
```

4.16.3. External Style Sheets

- If several webpages adhere to the same styles. The styles must be repeated for every page using embedded styles.
- If all pages in the website adhere to the same Styles external style sheets are used.
- External styles are for whole website.
- All the styles are stored separately in a file using file extension ".CSS".
- Useful when all the pages adhere to same style.
  Ex. " demo.css "

```
BODY { background-color : #FFFCC;
Font-family : Arial }
A: link { color : #OOAAFF }
A: visited { color : #AABBCC }
P { font-style : italic }
```

The < LINK > element in < head > tag is used to link css file for a webpage

< link relation=" stylesheet "   href= " file.css " >

"First.html "

```
< html >
< head >
        < link href= " demo.css "  rel = " stylesheet " >
< / head >
< body >
Welcome to Hyderabad
< a href = " hyd.html " > click here < /a >
< p > Hyd is for … < /p >
< /body >
< /html >
```

"Sec.html"

```
< html >
< head >
< link href= " demo.css "  rel = " stylesheet " >
< / head >
< body >
Welcome to Secunderabad
< a href = " Sec.html " > click here < /a >
< p > Sec is for … < /p >
< /body >
< /html >
```

4.16.4. Style Classes

- Enables the creation of styles as style classes in external or embedded style sheets.
- Assign the class attributes of an HTML element to the name of the style class in order to apply a style specified in that style class to that HTML element.

- The two types of style classes are
    i. A universal style class starts with a dot operator (.) followed by the class name

       Ex: **< style >**

       Class name { class definition }

       < / style >

    ii. An element specific style class starts with the element name followed by a dot operator , which is followed by the class name

       Ex: **< style >**

       Element name. class name { class definition }

       < / style >

Ex:

```
<html>
        <head>
                <title> style classes </title>
                 <style type = "text/css">
                    body  { background - color : #fof8ff }
                     th . color { background - color : # 800000}
                       . green { background - color : # 008000}
                 </style>
            </head>
        <body>
                 <table  border = 2>
                     <caption> student Data </caption>
                   <tr>
                          <th class ="color"> Name </th>
                          <th class ="color"> Address </th>
                   </tr>
                   <tr>
                          <td class ="green"> A.Ramesh </td>
                          <td class ="green"> Hyd</td>
                   </tr>
                   <tr>
                          <td class ="green"> A.Suresh</td>
                          <td class ="green"> Warangal</td>
                   </tr>
                 </table>
            </body>
            </html>
```

4.16.5. Multiple Styles

```
<html>
    <head>
        <link rel = "stylesheet" href = "one.css">
         <link rel = "stylesheet" href = "two.css">
          <link rel = "stylesheet" href = "three.css">
    </head>
     <body>
          ---------
         ---------
       </body>
  </html>
```

- When multiple external styles sheets are used, cascading styles, a combination of styles for different HTML elements, result.
- If multiple files styles affect the same element, only the last one is used.

4.16.6. <marquee> Tag

- The HTML <marquee> tag is used for scrolling piece of text or image displayed either horizontally across or vertically down.

- The various specific attributes are
  - **behaviour** – Defines the type of scrolling (scroll, slide, alternate)
  - **bgcolor** – Defines the color of text
  - **direction** – Direction of scrolling the content (up, down, left, right)
  - **height** – Height of marquee (pixels or %)
  - **width** – Width of marquee (pixels or %)
  - **hspace** – Horizontal space around marquee (pixels)
  - **vspace** – Vertical space around marquee (pixels)
  - **loop** – The default value is INFINITE, marquee loops endlessly. (or any no)
  - **scrolldelay** – Defines how long to delay between each jump (in seconds)
  - **scrollamount** – Defines how far to jump (number)

    Ex:

```
<marquee direction = "up " height = 10
     width  = 300   loop = 10  scrolldelay = 3>
      Welcome to css
</marquee>
```

4.16.7. **<pre> tag**

- HTML <pre> tag is a block element, used to designate preformatted text.
- The text between <pre> tags has both its spaces and line break preserved and displayed in a fixed width font.

- The Attributes are
  - **width** – Designates maximum number of characters per line

  Ex :

```
    <pre>
  Welcome to HYD
  India is with Intellectual people
</pre>
```

4.16.8. JavaScript Event Handling

```
<!-- To access data from text feilds in Script    onclick
    and onreset events -->

<html>
<head>
<script    language="javascript"    type="text/JavaScript"    >
    function fun1()
{
var    x    =    parseInt(document.f1.t1.value);    var    y    =
    parseInt(document.f1.t2.value);         var         z         =
    parseInt(document.f1.t3.value);   var    p    =    (x+y+z)/3;
    document.f1.t4.value = p;
}
</script>
</head>
```

```
<body>
<form name="f1" onreset="confirm('Would you like to clear')"
    >
<center>
Marks in Sub1: <input type="text" name="t1" > <BR> <BR> Marks
    in Sub1: <input type="text" name="t2" > <BR> <BR> Marks
    in Sub1:<input type="text" name="t3" > <BR> <BR> Average
    is :<input type="text" name="t4"    >    <BR> <BR>
<input type="reset" name="r1" value="clear" >    
     
<input   type="button"    name="b1"    value="FindAvg"
    onclick="fun1()">
</center>
</form>
</body></html>
```

<!-- To send data through arguments to JavaScript function onclick and onreset -->

```
<html>
<head>
<script   language="javascript"   type="text/javascript"   >
    function find(a , b ,c)
{     var x = parseInt(a); var y = parseInt(b); var z =
    parseInt(c); var p = (x+y+z)/3;
document.f1.t4.value = p;
}
</script>
</head>
<body>
<form name="f1" onreset="confirm('Would you like to clear')"
    >
<center>
Marks in Sub1: <input type="text" name="t1" id="m1" > <BR>
    <BR> Marks in Sub1: <input type="text" name="t2" id="m2"
    > <BR> <BR> Marks in Sub1:<input type="text" name="t3"
    id="m3" > <BR> <BR> Average is :<input type="text"
    name="t4" id="res" >   <BR> <BR>
<input type="reset" name="r1" value="clear" >    
     
```

```
<input        type="button"        name="b1"        value="FindAvg"
    onclick="find(m1.value,m2.value,m3.value)">
</center>
</form>
</body>
</html>
```

```
<!-- To access element by id onclick ,onload , onmouseup
    ,onmousedown, onmouseover . background color change
    document.body.style.backgroundImage = "url('filename')"
    document.body.style.background ="#110022"-->
```

```
<html>
<head>
<script   language="javascript"   type="text/javascript"   >
    function fun1()
{
document.body.style.backgroundImage = "url('Jellyfish.jpg')"
}
function fun2()
{
document.getElementById("uname").focus();
}
</script>
</head>
<body  onload="document.body.style.background      ='#110022'"
    onmousedown="fun1()"
    onmouseup="document.body.style.background ='#EE1100'"
onmouseover="fun2()">
<form name="f1" >
<input type= "text" name="t1" id="uname" size=50> <br>
<input type="button" name="b1" id="100" value="click here"
onclick="alert('              Hi             '            +
    document.getElementById('uname').value)" ><br>
</form>
</body>
</html>
```

<!—accessing the checkbox status -->

```
<html>
<head>
<script language="javascript">
function fun1()
{
var x = document.getElementById("ch1").value;
alert("x value is " +x);
//returns on if no value field in checkbox. if selected
// returns the value field string of the checkbox

if(x=="cse")
{
document.writeln(" cse selected");
}
else
{
document.writeln(" cse Not Selected");
}
}
</script>
<body>
<form name="f1" >
<input type="checkbox" value="cse" id="ch1" onclick="fun1()"
    > CSE
</form>
</body>
</html>
```

<!–Handling the Radio buttons -->

```
<!DOCTYPE html>
<html>
<body>
<script    language="javascript"    type="text/javascript">
    function fun1()
{
document.getElementById('male').checked        =        true;
    document.getElementById('fem').checked       =       false;
    document.getElementById("div1").innerHTML     =     "Gender
    Selected " +"MALE";
}
function fun2()
{
document.getElementById('male').checked        =       false;
    document.getElementById('fem').checked        =        true;
    document.getElementById("div1").innerHTML     =     "Gender
    Selected " +"FEMALE";
}
</script>
<form> Gender :
<input   type="radio"   id="male"   onclick="fun1()">   MALE
      
<input type="radio"   id="fem" onclick="fun2()"> FEMALE
</form>
<div id="div1" > </div>

</body>

</html>
```

4.17. AJAX

4.17.1. What is AJAX?

- AJAX abbreviated as **A**synchronous **J**avaScript **A**nd **X**ML.
- AJAX is not a language for programming.
- AJAX exclusively employs a mix of:
    - • An integrated XMLHttpRequest object in the browser (to request data from a web server)
- JavaScript and DOM in HTML (to display or use the data)
- • The name AJAX is deceptive. Although XML may be used by AJAX apps to transfer data, plain text and JSON text are also frequently used.

- AJAX enables asynchronous updating of web pages by secretly exchanging data with a web server. This indicates that a web page can be updated in sections without requiring a page reload.

4.17.2. AJAX Works Flow

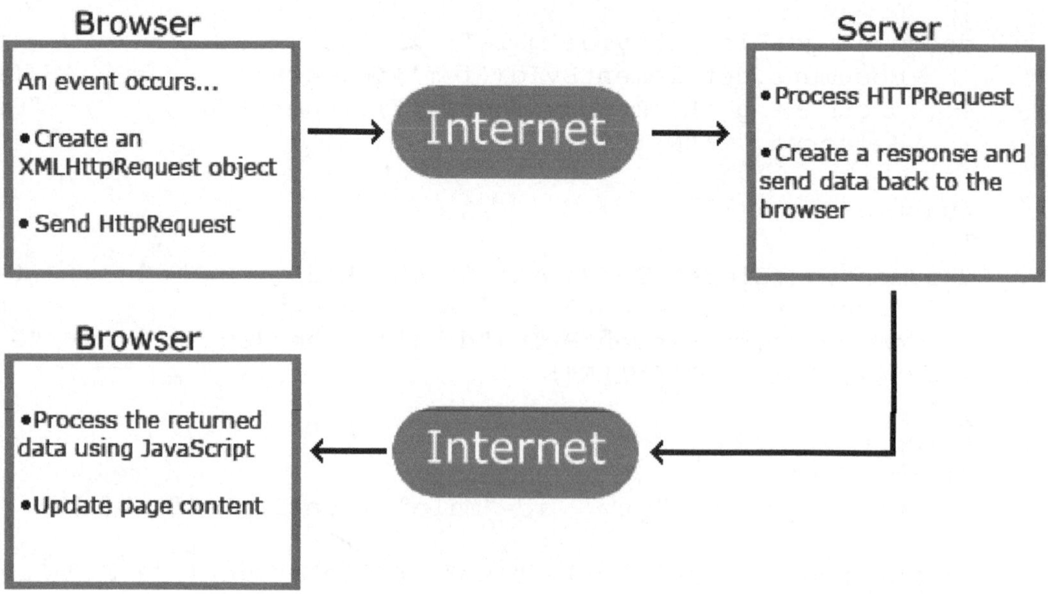

1. A web page contains an event (the page is loaded, a button is clicked)
2. JavaScript creates an object called XMLHttpRequest.
3. A web server receives a request from the XMLHttpRequest object.
4. The request is processed by the server
5. The web page receives a response from the server.
6. JavaScript reads the response
7. JavaScript carries out the appropriate action (such as page update).

4.17.3. How to Create a Web Application Using Ajax

- JavaScript is used by Ajax web applications to communicate with servers and update websites without reloading them.
- The eight steps that follow explain how to create a basic Ajax web application..

I. I. Find or create your data source URL. The page can only be updated by an Ajax web application when a server or other source of data that can be accessed through a URL is available. The following text, kept in a file called data.txt, will be used as an example.

```
Hello, World! This text is loaded using Ajax.
```

II. II. Produce your application's HTML. I've used a fundamental HTML5 template in the *following HTML, which has a h1 element* with an id attribute. Also, I developed a button that, when clicked, will activate the page's Ajax capability.

```
<html>
<head>
    <title>An Ajax Web Application</title>
</head>
<body>
    <h1 id="page-title"></h1>
    <button id="load-data">Click Here to Load
    the Data</button>
</body>
</html>
```

III. Add a script block to your HTML document (just after the closing body tag) and build an event listener to track button clicks.

```
<script>
document.getElementById("load-
    data").addEventListener("click",function(){
          });
</script>
```

IV. To request the data file, use an XMLHttpRequest object inside the event listener's callback method.

```
var xmlhttp = new XMLHttpRequest();
xmlhttp.open("GET", "data.txt");
```

V. With the onreadystatechange event handler, watch for a change in the xmlhttp response's state to find the response.

```
xmlhttp.onreadystatechange = function()
{
    //Do something here
}
```

VI. Write a callback function to insert the data from the text file into the h1 element when the state of the response changes.

```
xmlhttp.onreadystatechange = function() {
    document.getElementById("page-
    title").innerHTML = this.responseText; }
```

VII. Use the send() method to send the request.

```
xmlhttp.send();
```

- The finished HTML page should look like this:

```
<html>
<head>
    <title>An Ajax Web Application</title>
</head>
<body>
<h1 id="page-title"></h1>
<button id="load-data">Click Here to Load the Data</button>
<script>
    document.getElementById("load-
    data").addEventListener("click",function(){
      var xmlhttp = new XMLHttpRequest();
      xmlhttp.open("GET", "data.txt");
      xmlhttp.onreadystatechange = function() {
            document.getElementById("page-title").innerHTML =
    this.responseText;
      };
      xmlhttp.send();
    });
</script>
</body>
</html>
```

- Click the button on the HTML page after opening it in a browser. The script will display the following output in a browser:

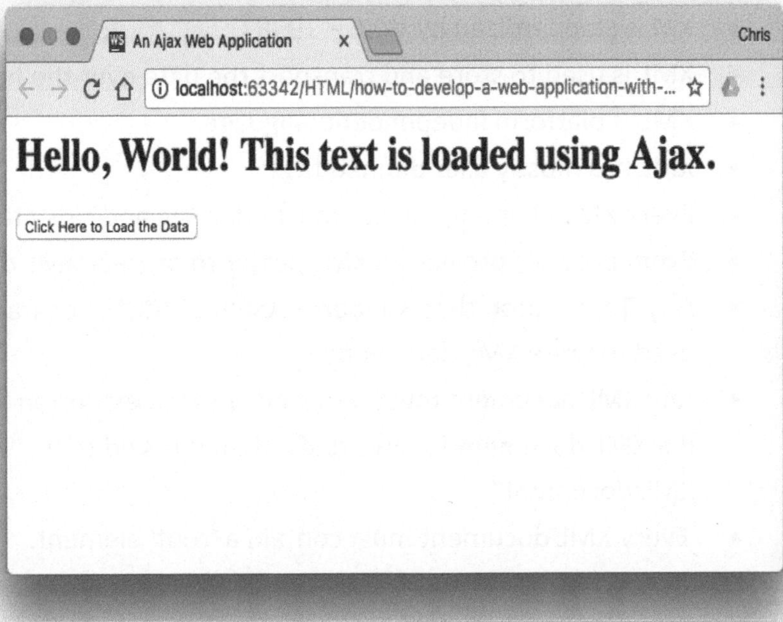

4.18. XML

4.18.1. Introduction to XML

- XML – Extensible markup language "XML is a markup language based on simple, platform independent rules for processing and displaying textual information in a structured way".

i. Applications of XML:-

- **XML** is used for various operations implementation
- Configuring information
- Publishing
- Electronic data interchange
- Voice mail system
- Remote method invocation (RMI)
- Object serialization
- Vector graphics
- XML is intended for transport or storage of data

- Every XML document contains XML elements and attributes associated with it.

ii. XML Characteristics

- XM is standardized by W3C – 1998
- XML is used to store and transport the data over the network.
- XML is platform independent language
- XML has mostly user defined tags
- Every XML element/tag has must open tag and close tag.
- Every browser provides a XML parser to process XML document.
- Any Text editor that supports ASCII/UNICODE character system used to write XML document
- Any XML document must be saved with file extension '.XML'.
- If a XML document follows rules, then it is said to be "well-formed XML document".
- Every XML document must contain a 'root' element.

HTML	XML
It is used to display or present data.	It is used to describe, store and transport data.
Most of the tags are predefined	Most of the tags are user defined.
It is case insensitive language	It is case sensitive
It will not check for syntax or rules	Checks for syntax and rules.
It does not preserves white spaces	It preserves the white spaces
Some of the tags are not closed. i.e., both container and non-container tag.	All the tags must have open and close tag.

iii. Features of XML/ Advantages of XML:-

- XML is intended for transport or storage of data
- XML allows, user is able to define and use own tags, called custom tags. It makes not require using only predefined tags defined by proprietary vendors.
- XML is for data storage, HTML is for presentation.
- XML allows user defined tags, HTML uses only predefined tags.
- XML contains only data and does not contain any formatting information.
- XML allows creating tags for any type of information like mathematical formula, employees data etc. These can be described using XML.
- XML document needs to be validated using external tools like DTD, schema.
- XML is not vendor specific or Browser Specific, but HTML is browser dependent.
- The manipulation of XML document, sorting, searching, rendering (presenting) is done using XSL. (Extensible style sheet language).
- The data can be in more than one application different applications perform different tasks on this data.
- XML is useful for exchanging data between different applications.
- XML document is human readable, we can edit by using simple text editors.
- XML document is language neutral, i.e. a java program can generate XML document and this document can be parsed/processed in PHP.
- XML document has a tree structure. Hence complex data can be arranged systematically and can understand in simple manner.
- XML files are platform independent, Hence can work on any platform.

iv. Comments on XML:-

<! ----

Specify the comments in multiple lines

--->

v. XML's objectives:-

- Users must have the ability to create and utilise their own tags. As a result, we are able to limit the use of a set of tags created by private vendors.
- Enables creation of a custom tag library based on website requirements.
- Enables setting formatting guidelines for user-defined tags.
- XML needs to support data storage or transmission.

4.18.2. XML documents

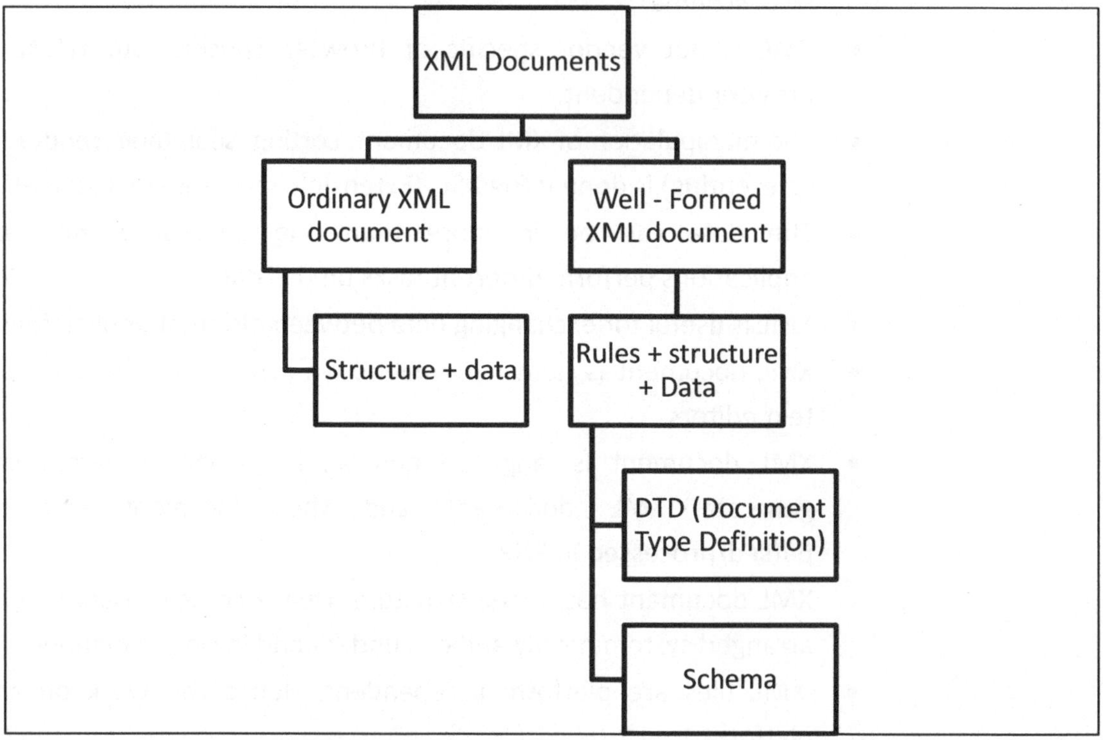

Example XML Document :-

```
<? Xml version = "1.0" encoding = "ISO- 8859-1"?>
<Product Data>
    <Product>
      <PID> P123 </PID>
      <PNAME> SAMSUNG A8 </PNAME>
      <DESCRIPTION> GOOD DISPLAY </DESCRIPTION>
<QTY> 5 </QTY>
</product>
 -------
--------        run      on      browser      as
    "c://demo/products.xml" (or) view XML document.
</Product Data>
```

i. Valid XML documents:-

- If an XML document has been validated using DTD or schema rules, it is valid.
- Then the document is also called well-formed XML document.
- A well-formed XML document must follow the following rules.

  I. Must have a starting tag and closing tag.
  II. XML tags are case sensitive
  III. XML elements must be properly nested
  IV. XML document must have a root element and only one root element.
  V. XML attribute values must be quoted. (single/double*) E.g: <emp title = "mr" > Raman </emp>*

- In XML white space is preserved. <emp> D Raman </emp>
- • A file's XML declaration must come first. The attributes of declaration is in the order version, encoding, standalone, etc.
- If XML declaration is done, version, must be specified, all other attributes are optional.
- XML elements can start with letter or ' – ' but not any other
- Element name cannot contain spaces.
- Element name cannot contain " : "
- Element name cannot start with "xml "in any case.
- No space after '<' char, but can have space before '>' closing char.
- To display special or ambiguous characters entities are used.

< (<), > (>), &quote; , & , '

- Example XML element names

  Ex: <emp>

  <_emp>

  <xml/emp>

  <emp-no>

  <emp1-no>

  <emp> & <emp> differs.

  <emp:name>

  </emp>

- Nested elements:-
- An XML element can contain other nested elements.

  Ex: <EMPNAME>

  <FIRST> Mohammad </FIRST>

  <MIDDLE> Yakub </MIDDLE>

  </EMPNAME>

- Empty elements:-
- An element may not have any content or nested elements in it.

  Ex: <MIDDLENAME/>

ii. Escaping delimiter characters:-

&	&
'	'
"	"
<	<
>	>

Ex: <DOB data = "< 12/07/2019 >"> </DOB>.

iii. XML Attributes:-

- Provides additional information about elements.

  Ex: <empno id = "ID021"> 1092 </empno>

iv. Example XML Documents:-

Products
  Product
  - Pid
  - Pname
  - Desc
  - Price
  - Qty

Emps
  Emp
  - Eid
  - Ename
  - DOJ
  - Dept
  - Sal

Catalog
  book
  - author
  - title
  - publisher
  - cost

//Example To Organize Employee Data

```
<?xml version="1.0" encoding="UTF-8" ?>
<emps>
<emp>
    <eid> 1001 </eid>
    <ename> Varsha</ename>
    <doj> 12/10/2016 </doj>
    <dept> Developer </dept>
    <sal> 85000 </sal>
</emp>
<emp>
    <eid> 1002</eid>
    <ename>Harsha</ename>
    <doj> 1/5/2017</doj>
    <dept> Designer </dept>
    <sal> 65000 </sal>
</emp>
<emp>
    <eid> 1092</eid>
    <ename>Teja</ename>
    <doj> 11/05/2015</doj>
    <dept> Tester </dept>
    <sal> 55000 </sal>
</emp>
</emps>
```

//Example To Organize Product Information

```
<?xml version="1.0" encoding="UTF-8" ?>
<PRODUCTS>
    <PRODUCT>
     <PID> S123 </PID>
     <PNAME>SAMSUNG A20 </PNAME>
     <DESC>This has High Quality Display </DESC>
     <PRICE>19000</PRICE>
     <QTY> 10 </QTY>
    </PRODUCT>
    <PRODUCT>
     <PID> S516 </PID>
     <PNAME>iPhone8</PNAME>
     <DESC>This will do all perfect</DESC>
     <PRICE>125000</PRICE>
     <QTY> 4 </QTY>
    </PRODUCT>
    <PRODUCT>
     <PID> S778 </PID>
     <PNAME>OPPO</PNAME>
     <DESC>Selfie Camera</DESC>
     <PRICE>25000</PRICE>
     <QTY> 8 </QTY>
    </PRODUCT>
</PRODUCTS>
```

4.18.3. Document Type Definition (DTD)

- In an XML document, the DTD is used to specify the guidelines and properties for using tags.
- An XML document can be defined as:
    I. Well-formed: The XML document is considered well-formed if it follows all standard XML criteria, including those requiring tags to be properly nested, opening and closing tags to be balanced, and empty tags to terminate with a '/>'.

II. An XML document with proper syntax is one that is well-formed. OR

- Valid: An XML document said to be valid when it is not only well-formed, but it also conforms to available DTD that specifies which tags it uses, what attributes those tags can contain, and which tags can occur inside other tags, among other properties.
- If a XML document follows the rules given by the DTD then the document is valid xml document.
- A well formed XML document can be validated against DTD or Schema.
- A DTD defines the XML document structure with a list of legal elements and attributes.
- A DTD defines the structure of XML document like elements and their relation, hierarchy, attributes and entities.
- DTDs check the validity of structure and vocabulary of an XML document against the grammatical rules of the appropriate XML language.

I. A DTD describes (Features)

- The elements that can appear in an XML document.
- The order in which the elements can appear.
- Optional and mandatory elements.
- Element attributes and whether they are optional or mandatory.
- Whether attributes can have default values.
- The set of rules for a XML document can be specified using DTD Types as

i. Inline or Internal DTD:

- The structure and rules of XML document are specified in the XML document.
- A DTD is referred to as an internal DTD if elements are declared within the XML files.
- To reference it as internal DTD, standalone attribute in XML declaration must be set to yes. This means the declaration works independent of external source.
- The syntax of internal DTD is:
  <!DOCTYPE root-element [element-declarations]>

ii. **External DTD:**

- The structure and rules of XML document are specified in a separate file with ".dtd" extension, referenced in XML document.
- In external DTD elements are declared outside the XML file. They are accessed by specifying the system attributes which may be either the legal .dtd file or a valid URL.
- To reference it as external DD, standalone attribute in the XML declaration must be set as no. This means, declaration includes information from the external source.
- Following is the syntax for external DTD:
  <!DOCTYPE root-element SYSTEM "file-name/URL">

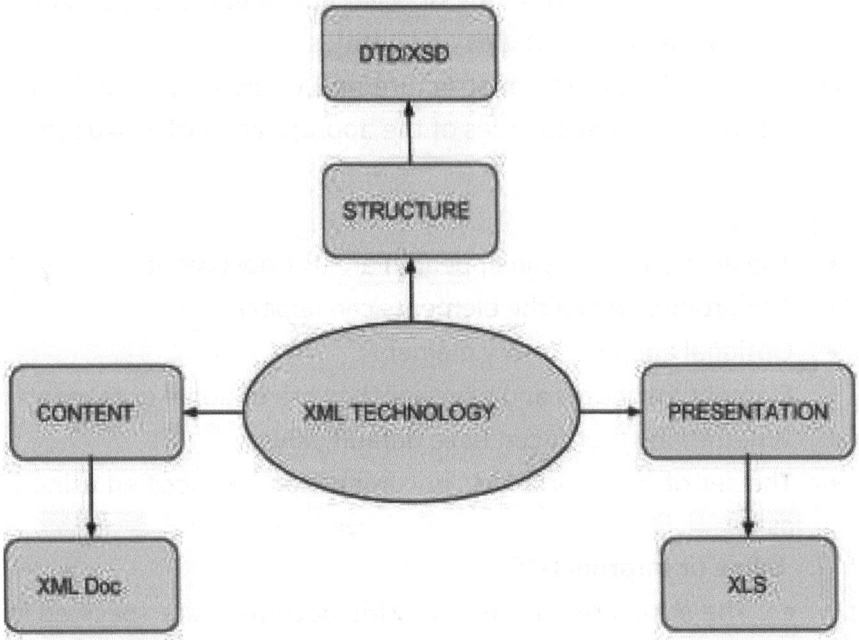

II. Advantages of using DTD

- Documentation - We can define own format for the XML files. Looking at this document a user/developer can understand the structure of the data.

- Validation - It gives a way to check the validity of XML files by checking whether the elements appear in the right order, mandatory elements and attributes are in place, the elements and attributes have not been inserted in an incorrect way, and so on.

III. Drawbacks of using DTD

- Namespace support is not available. The mechanism of namespace allows for the assignment of element and attribute names to groups. Yet in a DTD, namespaces must be defined inside the DTD, which goes against the intent of utilising namespaces.
- Only the text string data type is supported. (does not support datatypes).
- It lacks classes and objects. Hence, the DTDs cannot use the inheritance idea.
- Few options for expressing an element's cardinality.
- DTD will not use XML syntax, hence certain xml processors and xml frameworks do not understand DTD.
- DTD will not use namespaces.
- DTD Components / DTD Elements
    I. Elements (<!ELEMENT>)
    II. Attributes (<!ATTLIST>)
    III. Entities (<!ENTITY>)

IV. Defining Elements and Structure (<!ELEMENT>)

- • The building components of an XML document are known as XML elements. Elements can function as a container for text, elements, attributes, media objects, or a combination of all of these.
- • Every XML document consists of one or more elements, the limits of which are either defined by start-tags and end-tags or by empty elements.
- A DTD element is declared with an ELEMENT declaration. When an XML file is validated by DTD,
- Parser initially checks for the root element and then the child elements are validated.

  Syntax : **<!ELEMENT elementname (content)>**

<!ELEMENT elementname EMPTY > //Empty Element

Ex: <!ELEMENT address EMPTY>

- The XML element in XML file should be <address/>

  <!ELEMENT elementname (child1, child2...)> //Child Elements

  Ex: <!ELEMENT PRODUCT(PID,PNAME,DESC,PRICE,QTY)>

  <!ELEMENT elementname (#PCDATA)> //Element containing data

  Ex: <!ELEMENT PNAME (#PCDATA)>

  <!ELEMENT elementnam e (#PCDATA|child1|child2) > //Mixed type element

  <!ELEMENT address (#PCDATA|home | office)*>

- The Qualifiers for DTD definition are

Qualifier	Meaning
?	Optional , Zero or One occurrence <!ELEMENT address name?>
*	Zero or more Occurrences <!ELEMENT address name * >
+	one or more Occurrences <!ELEMENT address name + >
,	sequence of child elements separated by comma <!ELEMENT address (name, company, phone)>
|	It enables decision-making in the child element. <!ELEMENT address (home | office)>

<!ELEMENT PRODUCTS (PRODUCT+)> //root element
<!ELEMENT PRODUCT(PID,PNAME,DESC,PRICE,QTY)> //nested elements
<!ELEMENT PID(#PCDATA)> //element containing data
<!ELEMENT PNAME(#PCDATA)>
<!ELEMENT DESC(#PCDATA)>
<!ELEMENT PRICE(#PCDATA)>
<!ELEMENT QTY(#PCDATA)>

V. Defining DTD Attributes (<!ATTLIST>)

- An attribute defines a property of an element and provides additional information about that element.
- A name-value pair serves as the exclusive format for XML attributes..
- An element may have a variety of distinct properties.
- For each element, we declare a list of permitted attributes.
- All attributes are defined using ATTLIST declaration.
- The DTD attributes declaration's basic syntax is:
  <!ATTLIST element-name attribute-name attribute-type attribute-value>
- We want specify that an attribute is required.
  Ex: <!ATTLIST name id CDATA #REQUIRED>
  <!ATTLIST element-name attribute-name attribute-type "default-value">
  Ex: <!ATTLIST name id CDATA "0">

<!ATTLIST element-name attribute-name attribute-type #FIXED "value" >

#FIXED When you want to declare that the attribute value is fixed and cannot be altered, you use the keyword fixed followed by the value. Version numbers are a typical application of fixed properties.
Ex: <!ATTLIST company name #FIXED "INFOSYS">

<!ATTLIST element-name attribute-name attribute-type #IMPLIED>

- We must indicate that an attribute is implied if it has no necessary value, no fixed value, and no default value.
- Keyword #IMPLIED is used to specify an attribute as implied.
  Ex: <!ATTLIST name id CDATA #IMPLIED>
- PCDATA -> The PCDATA text is parsed by The XML parser. (Parsed Character Data)
- CDATA -> The text inside CDATA is ignored by the XML Parser. Unparsed character data. (A text string).
- # -> indicates the string followed by it is a special keyword not xml element name.
  enumeration -> Set of Enumerated values.

VI. Defining DTD Entities (!ENTITY)

- Entities are used to substitute a value for an XML element.
- Entities are a mechanism to define replacement values
- XML supports User defined entities or Predefined entities (<).
- • Entities may be externally or internally declared.

I. Internal Entity

- If an entity is declared within a DTD it is called as internal entity.
- Following is the syntax for internal entity declaration:
  <!ENTITY entity_name "entity_value">
  Ex: <!ENTITY phone_no "(011) 123-4567">
  <address> &phone_no; </address>

II. External Entity

- • An external entity is one that is declared outside of a DTD. Use either system IDs or public identifiers to relate to an external entity.
- Following is the syntax for External Entity declaration:
  <!ENTITY *name* SYSTEM "URI/URL">
  <!DOCTYPE books SYSTEM “books.dtd” [
  <!ENTITY copyright SYSTEM “copy.xml”> //external
  <!ENTITY call-us “123456789”>] > //internal0

VII. Inline or Internal DTD Examples

<!—Employees Info Using Inline or Internal DTD ⍰

```
<?xml version="1.0" encoding="UTF-8" standalone="no" ?>
<!DOCTYPE emps [
<!ELEMENT emps (emp+) >
<!ELEMENT emp (id,name,sal,dept,company)>
<!ELEMENT id (#PCDATA)>
<!ELEMENT name (#PCDATA)>
<!ELEMENT sal (#PCDATA)>
<!ELEMENT dept (#PCDATA)>
<!ELEMENT company (#PCDATA)>
<!ATTLIST dept grade CDATA #REQUIRED block CDATA "A">
<!ATTLIST id prefix CDATA #IMPLIED>
<!ENTITY address "Infosys Technoligies, Gachibowli, Hyderabad">
]>
```

```
<emps>
    <emp>
       <id prefix="INF">101</id>
       <name>Ramesh</name>
       <sal>85900</sal>
       <dept grade="B"> Developer</dept>
       <company>&lt;&address;&gt;</company>
    </emp>
    <emp>
       <id>121</id>
       <name>Suresh</name>
       <sal>65900</sal>
       <dept grade="C"> Tester</dept>
       <company>&quot;&address;&quot;</company>
    </emp>
    <emp>
       <id>131</id>
       <name>Ganesh</name>
       <sal>185900</sal>
       <dept grade="A">Designer</dept>
       <company>&apos;&address;&apos;</company>
    </emp>
</emps>
```

<!—Products Info Using Inline or Internal DTD □

```
<?xml version="1.0" encoding="UTF-8" standalone="no" ?>
<!DOCTYPE products [
<!ELEMENT products (product+)>
<!ELEMENT product (pid,pname,desc,price,qty)>
<!ELEMENT pid (#PCDATA)>
<!ELEMENT pname (#PCDATA)>
<!ELEMENT desc (#PCDATA)>
<!ELEMENT price (#PCDATA)>
<!ELEMENT qty (#PCDATA)>
]>

<products>
    <product>
       <pid> LG102 </pid>
       <pname> LG ULTRA HD 50 </pname>
       <desc> High Definition </desc>
       <price> 119000 </price>
       <qty> 12 </qty>
    </product>
```

```
    <product>
       <pid> SS110 </pid>
       <pname> SAMSUNG CURVE HD 50 </pname>
       <desc> High UV Definition </desc>
       <price> 139000 </price>
       <qty> 8 </qty>
    </product>

    <product>
       <pid> MI222 </pid>
       <pname> MI CURVE HD 50 </pname>
       <desc> High UV Definition </desc>
       <price> 69000 </price>
       <qty> 14 </qty>
    </product>

</products>
```

VIII. External DTD Examples

<!—Employees Info Using External DTD ?

```
emp.dtd
<!ELEMENT emps (emp+) >
<!ELEMENT emp (id,name,sal,dept,company)>
<!ELEMENT id (#PCDATA)>
<!ELEMENT name (#PCDATA)>
<!ELEMENT sal (#PCDATA)>
<!ELEMENT dept (#PCDATA)>
<!ELEMENT company (#PCDATA)>
<!ATTLIST dept grade CDATA #REQUIRED
block CDATA "A">
<!ATTLIST id prefix CDATA #IMPLIED>
<!ENTITY address "Infosys Technoligies, Gachibowli, Hyderabad">
empexter.xml
<?xml version="1.0" encoding="UTF-8" standalone="no" ?>
<!DOCTYPE emps SYSTEM "emp.dtd" >
    <emps>
       <emp>
          <id prefix="INF">101</id>
          <name>Ramesh</name>
          <sal>85900</sal>
```

```
            <dept grade="B"> Developer</dept>
            <company>&lt;&address;&gt;</company>
        </emp>
        <emp>
            <id>121</id>
            <name>Suresh</name>
            <sal>65900</sal>
            <dept grade="C"> Tester</dept>
            <company>&quot;&address;&quot;</company>
        </emp>
        <emp>
            <id>131</id>
            <name>Ganesh</name>
            <sal>185900</sal>
            <dept grade="A">Designer</dept>
            <company>&apos;&address;&apos;</company>
        </emp>
    </emps>
```

<!—Products Info Using External DTD ⍰

```
product.dtd
<!ELEMENT products (product+)>
<!ELEMENT product (pid,pname,desc,price,qty)>
<!ELEMENT pid (#PCDATA)>
<!ELEMENT pname (#PCDATA)>
<!ELEMENT desc (#PCDATA)>
<!ELEMENT price (#PCDATA)>
<!ELEMENT qty (#PCDATA)>
prodexter.xml

<?xml version="1.0" encoding="UTF-8" standalone="no" ?>
<!DOCTYPE products SYSTEM "product.dtd" >
    <products>
        <product>
            <pid> LG102 </pid>
            <pname> LG ULTRA HD 50 </pname>
            <desc> High Definition </desc>
            <price> 119000 </price>
            <qty> 12 </qty>
        </product>

        <product>
            <pid> SS110 </pid>
            <pname> SAMSUNG CURVE HD 50 </pname>
            <desc> High UV Definition </desc>
```

```
            <price> 139000 </price>
            <qty> 8 </qty>
        </product>

        <product>
            <pid> MI222 </pid>
            <pname> MI CURVE HD 50 </pname>
            <desc> High UV Definition </desc>
            <price> 69000 </price>
            <qty> 14 </qty>
        </product>

    </products>
```

<!—MotorBikes Info Using internal DTD ?

```
motorbike -> make,model,year,color,engine,chasis-num,accessories.
    engine -> eng-no,cylinders,fuel-type.
accessories attributes -> disk-brake => "yes or no" , auto-start
    =>"yes or no".
use appropriate entities.

<?xml version="1.0" encoding="UTF-8" standalone="no" ?>
<!DOCTYPE catalog [
<!ELEMENT catalog (motorbike*)>
<!ELEMENT                                                motorbike
    (make,model,year,color,engine,chasisnum,accessories)>
<!ELEMENT make (#PCDATA)>
<!ELEMENT model (#PCDATA)>
<!ELEMENT year (#PCDATA)>
<!ELEMENT color (#PCDATA)>
<!ELEMENT engine (eng-no,cylinders,fueltype)>
<!ELEMENT eng-no (#PCDATA)>
<!ELEMENT cylinders (#PCDATA)>
<!ELEMENT fueltype (#PCDATA)>
<!ELEMENT chasisnum (#PCDATA)>
<!ELEMENT accessories (#PCDATA)>
<!ATTLIST accessories diskbrake (yes|no) #REQUIRED>
<!ATTLIST accessories autostart (yes|no) #REQUIRED>
<!ENTITY mirror "TwoSides">
]>

<catalog>
    <motorbike>
        <make> HeroHonda</make>
        <model>PassionPro</model>
```

```
        <year> 2019</year>
        <color>Black</color>
            <engine>
                <eng-no> 2345EF</eng-no>
                <cylinders>2 </cylinders>
                <fueltype> Petrol</fueltype>
            </engine>
        <chasisnum>1122</chasisnum>
        <accessories diskbrake="yes" autostart="no"> ALL Reuired ,
            &mirror;</accessories>
    </motorbike>

    <motorbike>
        <make> Honda Active</make>
        <model>5G</model>
        <year> 2018</year>
        <color>RED</color>
            <engine>
                <eng-no> 12345EF</eng-no>
                <cylinders> 4 </cylinders>
                <fueltype> Petrol</fueltype>
            </engine>
        <chasisnum>110022</chasisnum>
        <accessories diskbrake="yes" autostart="yes"> ALL Reuired
            , &mirror;</accessories>
    </motorbike>
</catalog>
```

4.18.4. Namespaces in XML

- **It is possible for two document types to share the same element name but have distinct interpretations and meanings.**
- **We may distinguish between the elements and attributes of various XML document types using namespaces when merging them into other documents or processing many documents at once.**
- **XML Namespaces offer a way to prevent element name clashes.**
- **In XML, element names are created by the developer. When attempting to combine XML documents from various XML applications, this frequently leads to a disagreement.**

Ex:

```
<student>
    <BTECH>
```

```
            <course> Computer Science </course>
            <age> 22 </age>
        </BTECH>
        <MTECH>
            <course> DataScience </course>
            <age> 24 </age>
        </MTECH>
</student>
```

- Here would be a name conflict for <course> and <age>, but the elements have different content and meaning.
- Name conflicts in XML can easily be avoided using a name prefix.

```
<student xmlns:ug="http://www.w3.org/2001/XMLSchema"
xmlns:pg="http://www.w3.org/2001/XMLSchema" >
   <BTECH>
      <ug:course> Computer Science </ug:course>
      <ug:age> 22 </ug:age>
   </BTECH>
   <MTECH>
      <pg:course> DataScience </pg:course>
      <pg:age> 24 </pg:age>
   </MTECH>
</student>
```

4.18.5. XML Schema

- An XML document's structure is represented by an XML Schema.
- The constituent parts of an XML document are defined using an XML schema.
- Another name for the XML schema language is XML Schema Definition (XSD) language.
- In 2001, W3C recommended it.
- Similar to a DTD, an XML Schema explains the structure of an XML document.
- A properly formatted XML document is referred to as "Well Formed."
- • An XML document is "Well formed" and "Valid" if it has been validated against an XML Schema".
- Elements, properties, and child elements are defined by XML Schema..
- Furthermore, it specifies the fixed and default values for components and attributes.

- Permits the use of data types by the developer.

Benefits and Features of XML Schemas

- • XML is used to write XML Schemas
- XML Schemas used XML Syntax
- XML Schemas can expand to include new features.
- XML Schemas handle several data types.
- Defining document content is simpler
- Setting data restriction parameters is simpler.
- Verifying the accuracy of data is simpler.
- Data conversion between various data types is simpler.
- Namespaces are supported by XML Schemas.
- With XML Schema, you can include a description of your XML files' format.
- Independent groups of people can come to an agreement on a standard for exchanging data using XML Schema.
- XML Schema allows us to validate data.
- There's no need to pick up a new language
- Schema files can be edited using the XML editor.
- Schema files can be parsed using XML parsers.
- The XML DOM allows for Schemas manipulation.
- With XSLT, we can transform Schemas.

I. XML Schema (XSD) Elements

- XSD elements can be divided into two categories.

i. Simple Types:

- An element has no child elements or attributes; it just has a value.
- Simple type elements are only used in conjunction with text.
- • The <xs:simpleType> tag is used to generate the simple type element.

  Ex: <age> 30 </age>

  <xs:simpleType name=”age” type=”xs:integer”/>

ii. Complex Types

- Child elements and attributes are part of an element.
- A complicated type serves as a holding area for additional element definitions. By doing so, you may give your XML

documents some structure by defining which child elements a given element may have.

- With <xs:complexType> the complex type element is constructed.

Ex: <address>
<name> Infosys </name>
<company> Hyderabad </company>
<phone> 1234056789 </phone>
</address>

```
<xs:element name = "address">
 <xs:complexType>
    <xs:sequence>
      <xs:element name = "name" type = "xs:string" />
      <xs:element name = "company" type = "xs:string" />
      <xs:element name = "phone" type = "xs:integer" />
    </xs:sequence>
 </xs:complexType>
<xs:element>
```

II. XML Schema (XSD) Data types

- The following data formats are supported by XML element schemas:
  - **i. string data type**
    - The data type "string" is used to describe elements with characters, lines, or white spaces.
    - The element may have fixed, initial, or default values.
      <xs:element name="ElementName" type="xs:string"/>
      <xs:element name = "company" type = "xs:string" />
    - The XML document's element needs to contain
      <company> Infosys </company>
  - **ii. numeric data type**
    - "Integer" or "decimal" can be used to define the numeric values for an element.
      <xs:element name="ElementName" type="xs:integer"/>
      <xs:element name=ElementName" type="xs:decimal"/>

<xs:element name="age" type="xs:integer"/>

- The XML document's element needs to contain
  <age> 25 </age>
  <xs:element name="avg" type="xs:decimal"/>
- The XML document's element needs to contain
  <avg> 85.95 </avg>

iii. date data type

- The "date" data type is used to define the date in an XML element.
- All three entries must be present, and the date format is yyyy-mm-dd.
  <xs:element name="ElementName" type="xs:date"/>
  <xs:element name="dob" type="xs:date"/>
- The XML document's element needs to contain
  <dob> 2012-05-10 </dob>

iv. time data type

- The "time" data type can be used to specify the time for an XML element.
- The time format is hh:mm:ss
  <xs:element name="ElementName" type="xs:time"/>
  <xs:element name="starttime" type="xs:time"/>
- The XML document's element needs to contain
  <starttime > 11:45:52 </starttime >

v. boolean data type

- The true or false value can be assigned to xml element using "boolean".
  <xs:element name="ElementName" type="xs:boolean"/>
  <xs:element name="flag" type="xs:boolean"/>
- The XML document's element needs to contain
  <flag > true </flag >

III. Default and Fixed Values for Simple Elements

- Simple components may have a set fixed value OR a default value.
- If no additional value is supplied, a default value is automatically assigned to the element.

- The default setting is as follows in this example "HYD":
  <xs:element name="city" type="xs:string" default="HYD"/>
- • The element is likewise given a fixed value by default, and we are unable to specify a different value.
- • The fixed value in the following example is "HYD":
  <xs:element name="city" type="xs:string" fixed="HYD"/>

IV. XML Schema (XSD) Indicators

- The XML Schema uses various indicators to control how the elements can be used in XML document.
  i. **Order Indicators.**
     - used to specify the document's XML elements' order.
  ii. **All indicator**
     - The <all> indicator states that each child element must only appear once and that it can appear in any sequence.
       • When using the <all> indication, the "minOccurs" indicator can be set to 0 or 1, but the "maxOccurs" indicator can only be set to 1.

```
<xs:element name="person">
<xs:complexType>
<xs:all>
<xs:element name="firstname" type="xs:string"/>
<xs:element name="lastname" type="xs:string"/>
</xs:all>
</xs:complexType>
</xs:element>
```

  iii. **Choice Indicator**
     - The choice> indicator indicates that just one of the child elements may occur.

```
<xs:element name="person">
<xs:complexType>
<xs:choice>
<xs:element      name="employee"    type="string"/>
<xs:element      name="member"      type="string"/>
```

```
</xs:choice>
</xs:complexType>
</xs:element>
```

iv. **Sequence Indicator**

- The < sequence> indicator dictates the order in which the child elements must appear.

```
<xs:element name="emp">
<xs:complexType>
<xs:sequence>
<xs:element name="eid" type="xs:string"/>
<xs:element name="ename" type="xs:string"/>
</xs:sequence>
</xs:complexType>
</xs:element>
```

v. **Occurrence indicators.**

- The frequency of an element can be determined using the Occurrence indicators.
- For both maxOccurs and minoccurs, the default value is 1.

vi. **maxOccurs Indicator**

- • The maximum number of times an element may occur is specified by the <maxOccurs> indication.
- maxOccurs="unbounded" specifies any number of elements included.
- The meta characters
  * => minOccurs=0 , maxOccurs="unbounded"
  o + => minOccurs=1 , maxOccurs="unbounded"
  ? => minOccurs=0 , maxOccurs="1"
  o

vii. **minOccurs Indicator**

- The minimum number of times an element may occur is specified by the <minOccurs> indication.

```
<xs:element name="person">
<xs:complexType>
<xs:sequence>
<xs:element name="full_name" type="xs:string"/>
```

```
<xs:element name="child_name" type="xs:string"
maxOccurs="10" minOccurs="0"/>
</xs:sequence>
</xs:complexType>
</xs:element>
```

viii. Group Indicators.

- To identify related sets of elements, group indicators are utilised.

V. Element groups

- The group declaration defines element groupings.

```
<xs:group name="groupname">
...
</xs:group>
Ex:
<xs:group name="persongroup">
    <xs:sequence>
        <xs:element name="firstname" type="xs:string"/>
        <xs:element name="lastname" type="xs:string"/>
        <xs:element name="birthday" type="xs:date"/>
    </xs:sequence>
</xs:group>
<xs:element name="person" type="personinfo"/>

<xs:complexType name="personinfo">
    <xs:sequence>
        <xs:group ref="persongroup"/>
        <xs:element name="country" type="xs:string"/>
    </xs:sequence>
</xs:complexType>
```

VI. Attribute groups

- The attributeGroup declaration defines attribute groups.

```
<xs:attributeGroup name="groupname">
...
</xs:attributeGroup>
```

Ex:

```
<xs:attributeGroup name="personattrgroup">
      <xs:attribute name="prefix" type="xs:string"/>
      <xs:attribute name="grade" type="xs:string"/>
</xs:attributeGroup>

<xs:element name="person">
      <xs:complexType>
            <xs:attributeGroup ref="personattrgroup"/>
      </xs:complexType>
</xs:element>
```

VII. XML Schema (XSD) Restricitons

- • Acceptable values for XML elements or attributes are defined by restrictions. Facets are limitations on XML elements.
- <xs:restriction> is used to specify the restrictions over data used for XML element.
- Restrictions on Values-Specifying range for an element.
- It uses base attribute to specify the type of value.
- minInclusive, maxInclusive are used.

```
<xs:element name="age">
<xs:simpleType>
<xs:restriction base="xs:integer">
<xs:minInclusive value="18"/>
<xs:maxInclusive value="120"/>
</xs:restriction>
</xs:simpleType>
</xs:element>
```

i. Restrictions on a Set of Values

- Use the enumeration constraint to limit the content of an XML element to a set of permissible values.

```
<xs:element name="branch">
<xs:simpleType>
<xs:restriction base="xs:string">
<xs:enumeration value="CSE"/>
```

```
<xs:enumeration value="IT"/>
<xs:enumeration value="ECE"/>
</xs:restriction>
</xs:simpleType>
</xs:element>
```

ii. **Restrictions on a Series of Values**

- To limit the content of an XML element to define a series of numbers or letters that can be used.
- We would use the pattern constraint.

```
<xs:element name="ename">
    <xs:simpleType>
        <xs:restriction base="xs:string">
            <xs:pattern value="([A-Z])*"/>
        </xs:restriction>
    </xs:simpleType>
</xs:element>

<xs:element name="gender">
    <xs:simpleType>
        <xs:restriction base="xs:string">
            <xs:pattern value="male|female"/>
        </xs:restriction>
    </xs:simpleType>
</xs:element>

<xs:element name="password">
    <xs:simpleType>
        <xs:restriction base="xs:string">
            <xs:pattern value="[a-zA-Z0-9]{8}"/>
        </xs:restriction>
    </xs:simpleType>
</xs:element>
```

iii. **Restrictions on Length**

- • We would utilise the length, maxLength, and minLength constraints to restrict the length of a value in an element.
  Ex: An element "password" with a restriction. The value must be exactly 8 characters:

```
<xs:element name="password">
  <xs:simpleType>
```

```
        <xs:restriction base="xs:string">
        <xs:length value="8"/> //exact no.of
            chars
        </xs:restriction>
    </xs:simpleType>
</xs:element>
```

Ex: a "password" element that has a restriction. The value must be between 5 and 8 characters in length:

```
<xs:element name="password">
    <xs:simpleType>
        <xs:restriction base="xs:string">
          <xs:minLength value="5"/> //minimum
              no.of chars
          <xs:maxLength value="8"/> //maximum
              no.of chars
        </xs:restriction>
    </xs:simpleType>
</xs:element>
```

VIII. XML Schema (XSD) Attributes

- Simple types have been declared for all attributes.
- Basic components are ineligible for attributes. An element is regarded as belonging to a complicated type if it has attributes. Yet, the attribute is always defined as a basic type.
  <xs:attribute> IS USED TO DEFINE ATTRIBUTES.
  The attribute syntax is defined as:
  <xs:attribute name="attributename" type="datatype"/>
  <xs:attribute name="grade" type="xs:string"/>
- The element in XML file should be assigned grade attribute as
  <student grade="first"> A.Ramesh </student>

- Attributes may have a default value OR a fixed value specified.
  I. A default value is automatically assigned to the attribute when no other value is specified.
     <xs:attribute name="lang" type="xs:string"
        default="EN"/>

II. A fixed value is also automatically assigned to the attribute, and we cannot specify another value.
<xs:attribute name="lang" type="xs:string" fixed="EN"/>
Optional and Required Attributes

- • By default, attributes are optional. Use the "use" attribute to indicate that the attribute is necessary.
<xs:attribute name="lang" type="xs:string" use="required"/>

IX. Examples on XML Schema

```
//Example student schema rules and structure.
<?xml version="1.0"?>
<xs:schema xmlns:xs="http://www.w3.org/2001/XMLSchema">
    <xs:element name="student">
        <xs:complexType>
            <xs:sequence>
            <xs:element name="name" type="xs:string"/>
            <xs:element name="rollno" type="xs:string"/>
            <xs:element name="course" type="xs:string"/>
            <xs:element name="avg" type="xs:string"/>
            </xs:sequence>
        </xs:complexType>
    </xs:element>
</xs:schema>

//Example student schema XML file.
<?xml version="1.0" ?>
    <student xmlns:xsi="http://www.w3.org/2001/XMLSchema-
    instance" xsi:schemaLocation="studsche.xsd">
            <name> A.Ramesh</name>
            <rollno>530</rollno>
            <course>CSE</course>
            <avg> 79</avg>
    </student>

//Example book schema rules and structure.
<?xml version="1.0"?>
<xs:schema xmlns:xs="http://www.w3.org/2001/XMLSchema">

<xs:element name="catalog">
   <xs:complexType>
       <xs:sequence>
```

```
        <xs:element ref="book" minOccurs="1" maxOccurs="unbounded" />
        </xs:sequence>
    </xs:complexType>
</xs:element>

<xs:element name="book">
<xs:complexType>
    <xs:sequence>
        <xs:element name="title" type="xs:string" minOccurs="1"
            maxOccurs="1"/>
        <xs:element name="author" type="xs:string" minOccurs="1"
            maxOccurs="1"/>
        <xs:element name="publisher" type="xs:string"
            minOccurs="1" maxOccurs="1"/>
        <xs:element name="pages" type="xs:integer" minOccurs="1"
            maxOccurs="1"/>
        <xs:element name="price" type="xs:decimal" minOccurs="1"
            maxOccurs="1"/>
    </xs:sequence>
    <xs:attribute name="course" type="xs:string" use="required"/>
</xs:complexType>
</xs:element>
</xs:schema>
```

//Example book schema XML.

```
<?xml version="1.0" ?>
<!-- <?xml-stylesheet type="text/css" href="books.css"?> -->
<catalog   xmlns:xsi="http://www.w3.org/2001/XMLSchema-instance"
    xsi:schemaLocation="books.xsd">
    <book course="cse" >
        <title>  Web Technologies </title>
        <author>Ramesh</author>
        <publisher>DreamTech</publisher>
        <pages>1200</pages>
        <price>450.50</price>
    </book>


    <book course="cse">
        <title>  Operating Systems </title>
        <author>Galvin</author>
        <publisher>TMcH</publisher>
        <pages>900</pages>
        <price>850.50</price>
    </book>
    <book course="ece">
```

```
        <title>  Control Systems </title>
        <author>Davind Herny</author>
        <publisher>BPB</publisher>
        <pages>600</pages>
        <price>1250.70</price>
    </book>
</catalog>
```

```
//Example book styles in css.
title {font-family:serif;color:green;font-size:18pt} author{font-
    family:arial;color:red;font-size:12pt}        publisher{font-
    family:arial;color:blue;font-size:12pt}           pages{font-
    family:arial;color:red;font-size:12pt}            price{font-
    family:arial;color:blue;font-size:12pt}
```

4.19. XSLT

- The extensible stylesheet language, or XSL, is used to style XML documents.
- XSLT used for XSL Transformations.
- XSLT is a new language for transforming XML documents.
- Extensible Stylesheet Language Transformation commonly known as XSLT is a procedure to transform the XML document into other formats such as XHTML.
- XSLT, Extensible Stylesheet Language Transformations, have the ability to transform XML data from one format to another automatically.

4.19.1. Automatic conversion of XML file to a HTML page

- An XSLT stylesheet is used to define how the transformation rules to be applied on the target XML document. XSLT stylesheet is written in XML format.
- XSLT Processor takes the XSLT stylesheet and applies the transformation rules on the target XML document and then it generates a formatted document in the form of XML, HTML, or text format.
- This formatted document is then utilized by XSLT formatter to generate the actual output which is to be displayed to the end-user.

4.19.2. Advantages

- The advantages of using XSLT are:
- Not dependent on programming. Transformations are written in a separate XSL file, which is itself an XML document.
- • The transformations in the xsl file can be changed to change the output. No codes should be changed. Hence, web designers can alter the CSS and rapidly see the results of their changes.
- • Formatting is accomplished with HTML tags. These will not be processed by XSLT, and the browser will just render them.
- • <xsl:stylesheet> - XSL stylesheet declaration utilising an XSL namespace: Namespace informs the XLST processor which elements are utilised exclusively for output and which ones must be processed.

  ```
  <xsl:stylesheet version = "1.0"
  xmlns:xsl = "http://www.w3.org/1999/XSL/Transform">
  ```
- <xsl:template> - template tells the xlst processor about the section of xml document which is to be formatted. It takes an XPath expression. In general, it is matching document root element and will tell processor to process the entire document with this template.
- Defines a way to reuse templates in order to generate the desired output for nodes of a particular type/context.

  ```
  <xsl:template match = "/">
  ```
- <xsl:value-of> tag puts the value of the selected node as per expression as text.

  ```
  <xsl:value-of select = "firstname"/>
  ```
- <xsl:for-each> tag applies a template repeatedly for each node. processing instruction looks for each element matching the XPath expression

  ```
  <xsl:for-each select = "class/student">
  ```
- <xsl:sort> tag specifies a sort criteria on the nodes.

  ```
  <xsl:sort select = "firstname"/>
  ```
- <xsl:if> tag specifies a conditional test against the content of nodes.

  ```
  <xsl:if test = "marks > 60">
  ```

  The <xsl:choose> tag, in conjunction with the <xsl:otherwise> and <xsl:when> elements, specifies a number of conditional checks against the content of nodes.<xsl:choose>

```
        <xsl:when test = "marks >= 70"> Distinction
        </xsl:when>
        <xsl:otherwise> Fail
        </xsl:otherwise>
    </xsl:choose>
```

- <xsl:key> tag element specifies a named name-value pair assigned to a specific element in an XML document.

```
l:for-each select = "key('firstname-search', 'ramesh')">
```

- <message> tag element aids in the XSLT processing's debugging. It resembles alerts from javascript. <xsl:> Tag buffers a message to the XSLT processor, which stops the processing and sends a message to the calling application so that the error message can be displayed.

```
<xsl:if test = "firstname = ''">
<xsl:message terminate = "yes">A first name field is
empty.
</xsl:message>
</xsl:if>
```

//Example to Present Book Catalog – book.xml

```
<?xml version="1.0" encoding="UTF-8" standalone="no"?>
<?xml-stylesheet type = "text/xsl" href ="mystyle1.xsl" ?>
<catalog>
    <book>
       <title> XML for Web</title>
       <author>Winston</author>
       <publication>Pearson</publication>
       <edition>8</edition>
       <price>932Rs</price>
    </book>

    <book>
       <title> XML for Web</title>
       <author>Winston</author>
       <publication>Pearson</publication>
       <edition>8</edition>
       <price>932Rs</price>
    </book>
    <book>
       <title> XML for Web</title>
       <author>Winston</author>
       <publication>Pearson</publication>
```

```
        <edition>8</edition>
        <price>932Rs</price>
    </book>
    <book>
        <title> XML for Web</title>
        <author>Winston</author>
        <publication>Pearson</publication>
        <edition>8</edition>
        <price>932Rs</price>
    </book>
    <book>
        <title> XML for Web</title>
        <author>Winston</author>
        <publication>Pearson</publication>
        <edition>8</edition>
        <price>932Rs</price>
    </book>
</catalog>
```

//mystyle1.xsl

```
<?xml version="1.0" encoding="UTF-8"?>
<xsl:stylesheet  xmlns:xsl="http://www.w3.org/1999/XSL/Transform"
    version="1.0">
<xsl:template match="/">
    <html>
        <body>
            <table align="center" border="1">
                <caption> <h2>Books Information</h2></caption>
                <tr bgcolor="#BBEEFF">
                  <th style="text-align:left">Title</th>
                  <th style="text-align:left">Author</th>
                  <th style="text-align:left">Publication</th>
                  <th style="text-align:left">Edition</th>
                  <th style="text-align:left">Price</th>
                </tr>
                <xsl:for-each select="catalog/book">
                <tr>
                  <td><xsl:value-of select="title"/></td>
                  <td><xsl:value-of select="author"/></td>
                  <td><xsl:value-of
                      select="publication"/></td>
                  <td><xsl:value-of select="edition"/> </td>
                  <td><xsl:value-of select="price"/></td>
                </tr>
                </xsl:for-each>
```

```
            </table>
        </body>
    </html>
</xsl:template>
</xsl:stylesheet>
```

//Example to Present Student Information student.xml

```
<?xml version = "1.0"?>
<?xml-stylesheet type = "text/xsl" href = "studstyle.xsl"?>
<class>

    <student rollno = "561">
          <firstname>Rohith</firstname>
          <lastname>reddy</lastname>
          <marks>85</marks>
    </student>

    <student rollno = "573">
          <firstname>Vaneet</firstname>
          <lastname>Rao</lastname>
          <marks>55</marks>
    </student>
    <student rollno = "593">
          <firstname>ramesh</firstname>
          <lastname>kumar</lastname>
          <marks>64</marks>
    </student>
    <student rollno = "533">
          <firstname>Kushal</firstname>
          <lastname>swaroop</lastname>
          <marks>44</marks>
    </student>
</class>
```

//studstyle.xsl

```
<?xml version = "1.0" encoding = "UTF-8"?>

<xsl:stylesheet version = "1.0"
xmlns:xsl = "http://www.w3.org/1999/XSL/Transform">
<xsl:template match = "/">

<html>
<body>
<h2>Students</h2>
```

```
    <table border = "1">
    <tr bgcolor = "#9acd32">
        <th>Roll No</th>
        <th>First Name</th>
        <th>Last Name</th>
        <th>Marks</th>
    </tr>

<xsl:for-each select="class/student">
<tr>
    <!-- @ is used to access attribute -->
    <td><xsl:value-of select = "@rollno"/></td>
    <td><xsl:value-of select = "firstname"/></td>
    <td><xsl:value-of select = "lastname"/></td>
    <td><xsl:value-of select = "marks"/></td>
</tr>

</xsl:for-each>

</table>
</body>
</html>
</xsl:template>
</xsl:stylesheet>
```

//sorting data based on particular element (sort)-stud.xsl

```
<?xml version = "1.0" encoding = "UTF-8"?>
<xsl:stylesheet version = "1.0"
xmlns:xsl = "http://www.w3.org/1999/XSL/Transform">
<xsl:template match = "/">
<html>
    <body>
       <h2>Students</h2>
       <table border = "1">
           <tr bgcolor = "#9acd32">
               <th>Roll No</th>
               <th>First Name</th>
               <th>Last Name</th>
               <th>Marks</th>
           </tr>

           <xsl:for-each select = "class/student">

           <xsl:sort select = "firstname"/>
```

```
            <tr>
                <td><xsl:value-of select = "@rollno"/></td>
                <td><xsl:value-of select = "firstname"/></td>
                <td><xsl:value-of select = "lastname"/></td>
                <td><xsl:value-of select = "marks"/></td>
            </tr>
            </xsl:for-each>
        </table>
    </body>
</html>
</xsl:template>
</xsl:stylesheet>
```

//selecting data based on condition (if)-stud.xsl

```
<?xml version = "1.0" encoding = "UTF-8"?>
<xsl:stylesheet version = "1.0"
xmlns:xsl = "http://www.w3.org/1999/XSL/Transform">
    <xsl:template match = "/">
      <html>
        <body>
            <h2>Students</h2>
            <table border = "1">
                <tr bgcolor = "#9acd32">
                    <th>Roll No</th>
                    <th>First Name</th>
                    <th>Last Name</th>
                    <th>Marks</th>
                </tr>

                <xsl:for-each select = "class/student">

                    <xsl:if test = "marks > 60">
                       <tr>
                         <td><xsl:value-of select = "@rollno"/>
                             </td>
                         <td><xsl:value-of select = "firstname"/>
                             </td>
                         <td><xsl:value-of select = "lastname"/>
                             </td>
                         <td><xsl:value-of select = "marks"/></td>
                       </tr>
                    </xsl:if>
                </xsl:for-each>

            </table>
```

```
        </body>
      </html>
    </xsl:template>
</xsl:stylesheet>
```

//using choose, when otherwise-studstyle2.xsl

```
<?xml version = "1.0" encoding = "UTF-8"?>
<xsl:stylesheet version = "1.0"
    xmlns:xsl = "http://www.w3.org/1999/XSL/Transform">
    <xsl:template match = "/">
      <html>
        <body>
            <h2>Students</h2>
            <table border = "1">
                <tr bgcolor = "#9acd32">
                    <th>Roll No</th>
                    <th>First Name</th>
                    <th>Last Name</th>
                    <th>Marks</th>
                    <th>Grade</th>
                </tr>

                <xsl:for-each select = "class/student">

                    <tr>
                    <td><xsl:value-of select = "@rollno"/></td>
                    <td><xsl:value-of select = "firstname"/></td>
                    <td><xsl:value-of select = "lastname"/></td>
                    <td><xsl:value-of select = "marks"/></td>
                    <td>
                <xsl:choose>
                    <xsl:when test = "marks >= 70"> Distinction
                    </xsl:when>
                    <xsl:when test = "marks >= 60" > First
                    </xsl:when>
                    <xsl:when test = "marks >= 50" > Second
                    </xsl:when>
                    <xsl:otherwise> Fail
                    </xsl:otherwise>
                </xsl:choose>
                </td>
                </tr>
                </xsl:for-each>
```

```
            </table>
            </body>
        </html>
      </xsl:template>
</xsl:stylesheet>
```

4.20. Introduction to Web Services:

- There are several ways to define a web service.:
    - It is a client-server application or a communication-related application component.
    - How two devices communicate with each other through a network.
    - It is a system of software for open machine-to-machine communication..
    - It consists of a group of standards or protocols for sharing data between two applications or devices.

- Let's understand it by the figure given below:

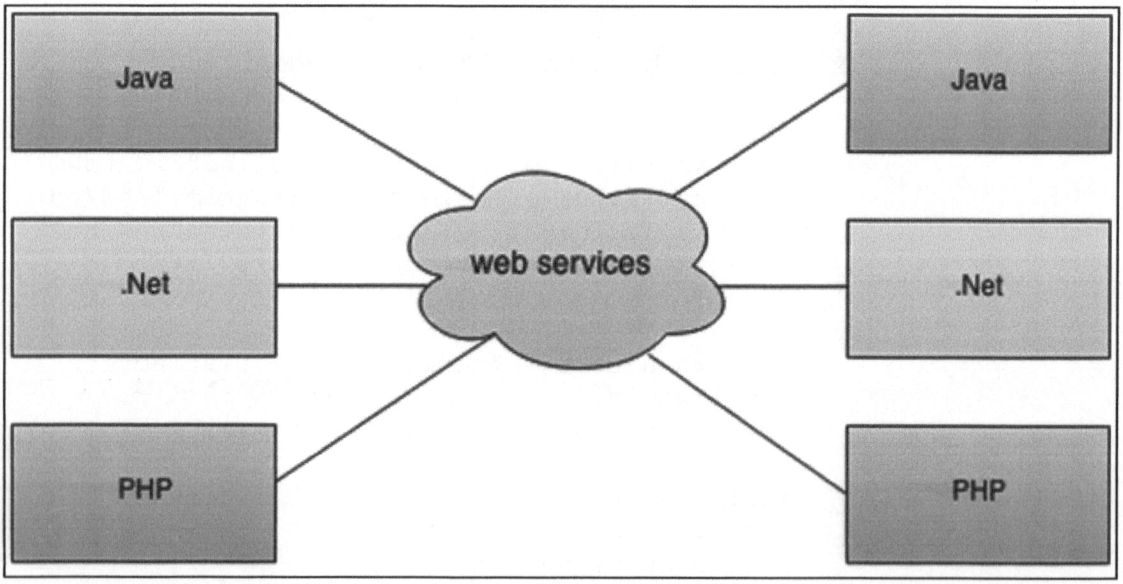

- Applications written in Java,.NET, and PHP can connect with one another across a network using web services, as shown in the image.

- The Java application, for instance, can communicate with Java,.Net, and PHP programmes. Web services are a language-neutral form of communication.

4.20.1. Types of Web Services

- The two primary categories of online services are.
    I. SOAP web services.
    II. RESTful web services.

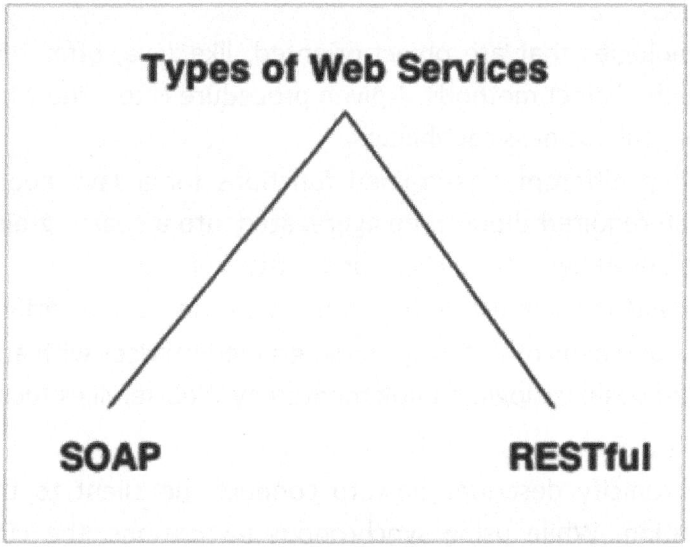

4.20.2. Web Service Features

i. XML-Based

- XML is used by Web services at the data definition and data transportation layers.
- Avoid any networking, operating system, or platform binding by using XML.
- Web services-based operations are very compatible at the fundamental level.

ii. Loosely Coupled

- A web service's client is not immediately fixed to the web service. Without compromising the client's capacity to communicate with the service, the web service interface may accommodate innovation over time.

- Operation based on Web services is fundamentally very interoperable.
- A system is said to be tightly linked if the client and server logic are closely intertwined, such that if one interface changes, another must also be updated.
- Software systems are typically easier to maintain and integrate with other systems when a loosely connected architecture is used.

iii. Coarse-Grained

- Technologies that are object-oriented, like Java, offer their functions through distinct methods. A given procedure is too finely tuned to offer any useful business capabilities.
- Creating different fine-grained functions for a Java application from scratch required them to be aggregated into a coarse-grained role that is then used by either a client or another service.
- Companies should use coarse-grained interfaces and verify them.
- A logical means of defining coarse-grained services with an appropriate level of business logic is implemented by Web services technology.

iv. Ability to be Synchronous or Asynchronous

- Synchronicity describes how to connect the client to the function's execution. While using synchronous invocations, the client waits to finish its service before moving on.
- Asynchronous operations enable a client to start a task before starting other operations.
- Synchronous customers receive their effects after the service has finished, while asynchronous clients fetch their results at a later time.
- In order to enable loosely linked systems, asynchronous functionality is crucial.

v. Supports Remote Procedure Calls (RPCs)

- Using an XML-based protocol, web services enable users to call procedures, functions, and methods on distant objects.
- A web service must support the input and output infrastructure exposed by remote systems.

- Enterprise component development Over the past few years, JavaBeans (EJBs) and.NET Components have increasingly been incorporated into architectural and enterprise deployments. Using a number of RPC protocols, both technologies are assigned and reachable.
- A web function can provide services on its own that are comparable to those of a traditional role or it can convert incoming calls into calls to an EJB or a.NET component.

vi. Supports Document Exchange

- • The ability of XML to represent complicated documents as well as data in a generic manner is one of its key advantages. These documents can be as straightforward as listing a current address or as complex as outlining an entire book or a Request for Quotation (RFQ).
- To facilitate company integration, Web services offer the transparent movement of documents.

4.20.3. Web Service Components

- There are three major web service components.
  - I. SOAP
  - II. WSDL
  - III. UDDI

i. SOAP

- The name Simple Object Access Protocol (SOAP) is an acronym.
- A web service access protocol based on XML is called SOAP.
- A W3C recommendation for application communication is SOAP.
- Since SOAP is XML-based, it is independent of language and platform. In other words, it may be utilised on any platform having the programming languages Java,.Net, or PHP.

ii. WSDL

- Web Services Description Language is known as WSDL.
- A WSDL is an XML document that contains details about web services, including the method name, method parameter, and access information.
- UDDI includes WSDL. It serves as an interface for web service programmes.

- WSDL is pronounced as wiz-dull.

iii. UDDI

- Universal Description, Discovery, and Integration is referred to as UDDI.
- UDDI is a framework for describing, finding, and integrating online services that is based on XML.
- UDDI is a directory of web service interfaces that contains data on web services and is described using WSDL.

Unit Summary

Through this unit we have learnt about JavaScript and objects, DOM and web browser environments. We have also understood Forms, validations in DHTML, AJAX, it's advantages & disadvantages. In addition we have delved into XML, It's usage, DTD and Schema, XSLT and It's Applications, comparison with XML and Introductory concepts of web Services.

EXERCISE

Multiple Choice Questions

1.1 JavaScript objects can be created with the new keyword, and with the .... function.

a) object()

b) object.create()

c) JavaScript.object()

d) create.object()

1.2 A .... object is any object created by the execution of JavaScript code.

a) native

b) host

c) user defined

d) remote

1.3 What will be printed in the console on execution of the following JS code:

```
var array = [1, 2, 3, 4, 5, 6, 7, 8, 9, 10, 11, 12, 13, 14, 15];
var myArr= array.filter(v => v % 3 === 0);
console.log(myArr);
```

a) myArr

b) [3, 6, 9, 12, 15]

c) [1, 2, 3, 4, 5, 6, 7, 8, 9, 10, 11, 12, 13, 14, 15]

d) [1, 2, 4, 5, 7, 8, 10, 11, 13, 14]

1.4. what will be the output of below code?

```
var val = "JavaScript String"
splittedVal = val.split('a',2)
console.log(splittedVal);
```

a) ['J', 'v']

b) ['J' ,'v','Script']

c) ['J', 'v', 'Script String']

d) ['JavaScript String']

1.5 what will be the output of below code?

NOTE: The code is executed on 2019-5-9

```
var todaysDate = new Date()
console.log( todaysDate.toLocaleString() );
```

a) 2019-05-09T09:29:53.181Z

b) 2019-5-9

c) 15:00:34

d) 2019-5-9 15:02:35

1.6 If para1 is the DOM object for a paragraph, what is the correct syntax to change the text within the paragraph?

a) "New Text"?

b) para1.value="New Text";

c) para1.firstChild.nodeValue= "New Text";

d) para1.nodeValue="New Text";.

1.7 JavaScript provides a special constructor function called Object() to build the object.

a) TRUE

b) FALSE

c) Can be true or false

d) Can not say

1.8 XML stands for ____.

a) eXtensible Margin Language

b) Xtensible Markup Language

c) eXtensible Markup Language

d) Xtensible Margin Language

1.9 XML is designed to ____ and ____ data.

a) design, style

b) design, send

c) store, style

d) store, transport

1.10 ____ is used to read XML documents and provide access to their content and structure.

a) XML Processor

b) XML Pre-processor

c) XML Compiler

d) XML Interpreter

1.11 Which is the correct XML declaration?

a) <xml version="1.0" encoding="UTF-8"/>

b) <xml version="1.0" encoding="UTF-8"></xml>

c) <?xml version="1.0" encoding="UTF-8"?>

d) <?xml type="document" version="1.0" encoding="UTF-8"?>

1.12 In XML, DTD stands for ____.

a) Document Type Declaration

b) Data Type Definition

c) Document Type Definition

d) Document To Declaration

1.13 Which is the correct syntax to link XML file with CSS?

a) <?xml type="text/css" href="file.css"?>

b) <?xml type="text/css" src="file.css"?>

c) <?xml-stylesheet type="text/css" href="file.css"?>

d) <?xml-stylesheet type="text/css" src="file.css"?>

1.14 What does SAX stand for ____.

a) Simple Application for XML

b) Safe API for XML

c) Super Application for XML
d) Simple API for XML

1.15 In XML DOM, what does DOM stand for ____.
a) Document Object Model
b) Date Object Model
c) Document Oriented Model
d) Document Open Model

1.16 What is the default type of 'type' attribute of <input> element?
a) Text
b) Password
c) Numerals
d) Special Characters

1.17 Which attribute is used for activation of JavaScript?
a) button
b) checkbox
c) url
d) submit

1.18 Which element is used to create multi-line text input?
a) text
b) text area
c) submit
d) radio button

1.19 Which attribute is not used for the radio type?
a) name
b) value
c) checked
d) selected

1.20 The basic Web Services platform is combination of _____ and _______
a) CSS + HTTP
b) XML + HTML

c) XML + HTTP

d) CSS + JAVA

Answers of Multiple Choice Questions

1.4 (b) 1.2 (c) 1.3 (c) 1.4 (a) 1.5 (d)1.6 (b) 1.7(a) 1.8 (c) 1.9 (d)1.10(a) 1.11(c) 1.12 (c) 1.13(c) 1.14(d) 1.15(a) 1.16(a) 1.17(a) 1.18(b) 1.19() 1.20(c)

Short and Long Answer Type Questions

Category I

1.1 Write a JavaScript program to list the properties of a JavaScript object Write the characteristics of Java Script?

1.2 Write a JavaScript program to calculate the area and perimeter of a circle?

1.3 Write a JavaScript program to set the background color of a paragraph

1.4 Write a JavaScript function that generates all combinations of a string

1.5 Write a JavaScript function that accepts a string as a parameter and find the longest word within the string.

1.6 Write the differences between valid and well formed XML?

1.7 Write about the web services?

Category II

1.8 Write a JavaScript function to check whether a given value is a DOM element?

1.9 Write the matrix multiplication program using Array Object in Java Script?Write a JavaScript program to sort a list of elements using Quick sort

1.10 Write a JavaScript program to calculate the volume of a sphere. Sample Output of the form :

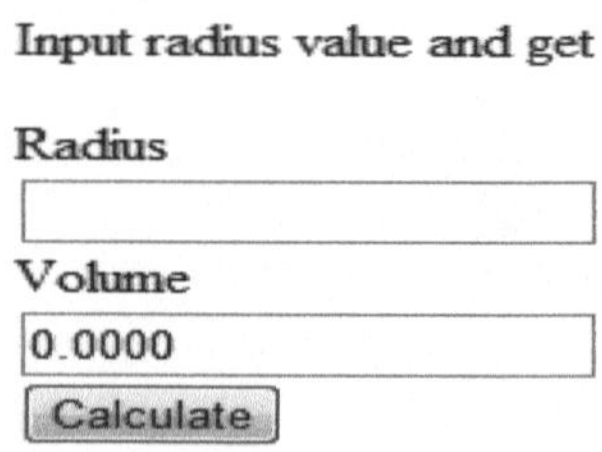

1.11 Write a JavaScript program to get the width and height of the window (any time the window is resized).

1.12 write a html program to control the background repetition of the image with background repeat property.

1.13 Write a program to perform client side validation in the following fields.

1. Username(should at least 6 characters)
2. Password(should at least 8 characters)

3. Mobile number
4. E-mail

1.14 Write a XML document to display the book information which includes the following XSL.

1. Title 2. Author 3. Publisher 4. Price 5. ISB number

References and suggested readings

1. Web Technologies: HTML, JAVASCRIPT, PHP, JAVA, JSP, XML and AJAX, Black Book by Kogent Learning Solutions Inc. | 28 November 2012
2. HTML 5 Black Book, Covers CSS 3, JavaScript, XML, XHTML, AJAX, PHP and jQuery, 2ed by DT Editorial Services | 1 January 2016
3. Head First JavaScript Programming: A Brain-Friendly Guide by Elisabeth Robson and Eric Freeman | 1 January 2014
4. XML: The Complete Reference by Heather Williamson | 9 July 2001
5. XSLT [Book] (oreilly.com)
6. J2EE™ Web Services, 1e by HAEFEL | 1 January 2004

Dynamic QR CODE for further reading

5 PHP

UNIT SPECIFICS

Through this unit we will discuss the following aspects:

- *Server-side scripting.*
- *Advance PHP Databases.*
- *Inserting and data by Connecting Server.*
- *Listing, Altering and Deleting Databases and Tables.*
- *PHP myadmin and database bugs.*

RATIONALE

This unit focuses on the server-side scripting and constructs in PHP like Arrays, functions and forms. Advanced PHP Databases will be explained by various example programs such as Connecting to the server with connection objects and discussed how to handle the situations where connection object is not established. mostly focuses on building databases, choosing databases, listing databases, listing table names, creating tables, adding data, changing tables, queries, deleting databases, deleting data, and deleting tables. flaws in PHP's myadmin and databases.

PRE-REQUISITES

Problem Solving Skills

Object Oriented Programming

UNIT OUTCOMES

List of outcomes of this unit is as follows:

U5-O1: Explain Server-side Scripting

U5-O2: Explain advanced PHP Databases

U5-O3: Explain the PHP Database Creation, Selecting and Listing.

U5-O4: Explain the PHP Table creation, inserting data into tables and deleting tables.

U5-O5: Describe the PHP myadmin and database bugs.

Unit-5 Outcomes	EXPECTED MAPPING WITH COURSE OUTCOMES (1- Weak Correlation; 2- Medium correlation; 3- Strong Correlation)				
	CO-1	CO-2	CO-3	CO-4	CO-5
U5-O1	3	3	3	2	1
U5-O2	2	2	2	3	1
U5-O3	2	2	2	3	1
U5-O4	2	2	2	3	2
U5-O5	2	2	2	3	2

Server Side Scripting

- It is a method of programming that creates the code needed to operate server-side software.
- Server-side scripting refers to any scripting or programming that can be executed on a web server.
- Script Code Created on the Server Computer
- For processing, server side scripting uses a server.
- A server-side script that users cannot see is running in the server end.
- Tasks such as website customization, dynamic content changes, user query response creation, database access, basic computation, etc.
- A communication channel between a server and client is built via server side scripting.
- The data and source code are more safe since the web server abstracts the scripts from the end user.
- Languages used for server-side scripting include PHP, Python, Ruby, JSP, ASP, ASP.Net, ColdFusion, and others.

5. Introduction to PHP

PHP - (Hypertext preprocessor) is a server side scripting language used to create dynamic webpages. Create dynamic webpages.

- Originally called personal Home page
- The various version of PHP are PHP version 2 – PHP version 6 (current)
- PHP scripts run on a server.
- PHP is a free and open-source programme.

- Developed by Apache group, in 1994.

5.1. PHP characteristics

- Server side scripting language
- Open source software
- Free to download and use. (www.php.net)
- Runs on different platforms. (windows, linux etc)
- Compatible with all the servers used today (Apache, IIs etc)
- Supports many databases (MySql, Oracle, Sybase, Postgre SQL etc)
- A PHP file includes scripts, HTML elements, and text.
- The browser receives HTML-formatted PHP files back.
- PHP files contain the ".php," ".php3," or ".phtml" extension.
- Mainly used for form handling & database access.
- Process script code in Interpreter & PHP Parser.
- PHP statements are terminated by semicolon(;)

5.2. Features of PHP

- PHP is a general purpose scripting language runs on a webserver.
- PHP creates dynamic website content by using script code as input.
- PHP can be installed on the majority of webservers and practically every platform and operating system.
- The main features of PHP are

I. **Access control** - gives access control configuration a built-in web-based configuration panel.**File Upload support** – PHP offers the MIME (multipurpose Internet mail Extension) decoding procedure for server-side file uploads. gives users the ability to upload files to a web server.

II. **HTTP – based Authentication control** - enables users to design unique authentication methods for web servers.

III. **Supports variables, arrays, Associative arrays.** can be transferred across websites utilising the GET and POST method types.

IV. **Conditional statements and loops**

V. **Extended regular expressions** - utilised for string manipulation, pattern substitution, and pattern matching.

VI. **Raw HTTP Header Control -** permits the transmission of a URL from one client to another. used to change the most recent header on websites

VII. **Access logging –** allows you to keep track of how often a website or page is accessed. Additionally, it assists in creating the footer that displays access information on every page.

VIII. **Safe mode Support –** allows several users to run PHP scripts concurrently on the same server. solves the security issue with shared servers.

IX. **Open source –** enables the user to work with many programming languages. The user can select a language to write their own source code for various applications and release it for free online.

X. **Third part application support -** includes a common API for database access and supports a large variety of various databases.

XI. **PHP Extensible Architecture –** allows users to send and receive emails using the SMTP Internet protocol in a variety of file formats, including GIF, JPEG, and PNG. access to Java classes, C libraries, etc.

XII. **Dynamic typing -** PHP does not require declaring variables. Only when a variable is assigned a value does its type become set.

XIII. **Large no.of library functions -** To write efficient PHP code.

5.3. Advantages of PHP over other scripting languages.

I. **Active server pages (ASP) –** support by only Microsoft IIS. (Internet Information server (IIS) used only for win 32 (windows) systems. ASP is much slower, less stable & less secure.

II. Supported by almost all the web servers. Works with apache, proven record of speed, reliability & secure.

III. **Cold Fusion -** Available only for win32, Solaris, Linux 7 HP, designed for the non-programmers, focused on programmers. Compared with cold fusion faster, more efficient & stable language.

IV. **Perl (Practical Extraction & Reporting language) -** Relatively PHP is Easier to integrate with HTML, easy to learn & has smaller learning curve. No prior knowledge of programming required. Perl is for complex tasks, more complicated.

V. **JSP (java server pages) -** PHP is supported for all platforms, that is equal or above 32 bits. But JSP is supported by only those platforms that have a JVM. Performance of PHP is 5 times faster than JSP.

5.4. Creating a PHP Script:

- **demo.php**

```
<html>
 <body>
      <?php
           echo " Introduction to PHP"
                echo " Welcome to server side scripting"
      ?>
 </body>
</html>
```

- The PHP file contains PHP instructions, JavaScript, HTML & CSS.
- On Browser **http://localhost/demo.php**
- After receiving the request, the webserver passes the PHP script on to the PHP Parser and Interpreter to continue processing.
- The interpreter reads script in <?php ...?>, executes them, passes the result back to server, the server sends the result back to the browser.
- 'echo' or 'print' statement used to display.
    - **i.** <? Php...?> tags must surround all PHP code.
    - **ii.** A semicolon must end each statement in PHP.
    - **iii.** The parser ignores blank lines in the script.// → single line comments, /* ... */→ Multiline comments.
    - **iv.** The PHP Parser identity's if any error.

5.4.1. Escape Characters:

- Used to display certain characters.
- \" → prints next character as double quote.
- \' → prints next character as single quote.
- \n → prints a new line character.
- \t → prints a tab character.
- \$ → prints a $ as next character.
- \\ → prints \ as a next character.
- \r →prints carriage return as next char.

5.5. PHP Variables

- Variables and Constants are used to store data to process programs.
- A variable has an identifier, value, scope and lifetime.

5.5.1. Naming Rules & Conventions

- Every variable must be preceded by '$' sign. Ex: $ sum, $name
- variable must start with either a letter or a underscore. Ex: $ _sum, $name,$123(wrong)
- variable name must contain alpha-numeric characters and underscores. No special characters allowed. Ex: $sum_60, $sum!=60 (wrong), $@name (wrong)
- The variable name should not contain spaces. More than one word, separate with an underscore/ capitalization. Ex; $cse avg (wrong), $cseAvg (correct), $cse_avg (correct).
- The length of variable name has no limit
- PHP variables are case sensitive.

5.5.2. Assigning values to variables:

- $ sum = 20;
- $ s = $ sum;
- $ s = $ s+1;
  Ex: $ x = 10;
  $ y = 20;
- echo $x, $ y; → echo statement allows multiple arguments separated by comma(,)
- → echo statement does not return a value.
- print $ x, $y; → not allowed, print statement doesn't take multiple arguments.
- print $ x; → Formatted O/P is possible only with print statement.

5.5.3. Assigning a value by Reference method:

- <? php
- $name = "welcome";
- $ str = &$name;
- $ str = "goodbye";
- echo $ str; // goodbye
- echo $name; //goodbye
- note: Do not assign expression to Reference variables.
- PHP allows to set the name of a variable dynamically, i.e.

```
$name = 'student_name'; //creates new variable
    ${$name} = 'ramesh';
    echo "$student_name; //ramesh
```

5.5.4. Destroying variables

- PHP allows to destroy variables or an array element when not required. unset() function is used to destroy the elements of array or variable.

  Ex:
  ```
  $name = "Hyderabad";
  echo "$name"
  unset($name);    //destroy var
  echo "$name";    //error.
  ```

5.5.5. Using Constants

- Constants are identifiers that store values, which cannot change during the execution of script.
- Constants are used for defining
  i. Configuration settings
  ii. Error codes and flags
- Constants are case sensitive.
- Constants identifier name is always in uppercase.
- Unlike variables, Constants names do not start with '$' sign.
- The naming convention is same as variables
- A constant name starts with a letter or underscore, followed by any no.of digits, letters (or) underscore.
- The syntax to create a constant is define("CONSTANT_NAME", constant_value);

  Ex: define("uname", scott);
- A constant can hold only a scalar value, where as a variable can store arrays or objects.

5.6. Exploring Data types in PHP:

- A datatype define the type of variables data, i.e. category of values.
  I. **Integers** – Represents a whole number with no fractional components. The range of integers varies from OS to OS. General range – 2147483648 to +2147483647. Integers also written in decimal, octal or hexadecimal.

II. **Floating point Numbers** - Represents real numbers that include decimal place.
   - Numeric floating point no(3.142)
   - Scientific notation (0.214E2) the notation is [num] e [Exponent].

III. **Strings** – Represents text literals of any length. Strings are enclosed in single quotes or double quotes. Ex: $name = "Hyderabad";
Name is Hyderabad ← echo "name is $name"
Name is $name ← echo "name is $name"

IV. **Booleans** – Represents a true or false value. All conditions return true/false based on the conditions tested. Returns always false for:-
   - Keyword false
   - Integer 0
   - Float 0.0
   - Empty string(" ")
   - String "o"
   - An object with no values/methods
   - The null value.

V. **Array** – Represents a variable that holds a collection of related data elements. Each element is accessed with index. Position is specified numerically or alphabetically.

VI. **Object** – Stores data and information to process the data. Objects are created by declaring a class.

VII. **Resource** – Stores references to functions and resources external to PHP.
Ex: A database call.

VIII. **NULL** – It can have only one value, null. Null is datatype and also a keyword literal when no value assigned to a variable, it is assigned to null.

- Variable in PHP are not necessary to specify the type, the type is assigned when a value is stored. Ex: $name = "Hyderabad"; //string
- Datatypes are divided as
  1) Scalar (or) Primitive data types : Integers, floating point nor, strings and Booleans
  2) Compound datatypes : Arrays, objects
  3) Special data types : Resources, NULL.

5.6.1. Datatype of a variable

- gettype() - is function used to return the datatype of a variable dynamically.
  Ex: $value = “Hyderabad”;
  echo gettype($value); //string
  unset($value); $value = “31.72”;
  gettype($value); echo gettype($value); //double
  echo gettype(0); //Null
  $value = 3
  echo gettype($value); // integer
- The Special Functions to Check Datatype:
  - `is_bool()` function is used to tests if a variable holds a Boolean value.
  - `is_numeric()` function is used to Tests if a variable holds a numeric value.
  - `is_int()` function is used to Tests if a var holds a integer.
  - `is_float()` function is used to Tests if a var holds a float .
  - `is_string()` function is used to Tests if a var holds a string .
  - `is_null()` function is used to Tests if a var holds a NULL.
  - `is_array()` function is used to Tests if a var is an array.
  - `is_object()` function is used to Tests if a var is an object.
- PHP is an object oriented scripting language it is open source and interpreted,.
- Used to develop dynamic webpages
- Executes script code on the server.
- PHP script executes much faster than other scripts
- Platform independent
- Compatible will all servers Apache, IIs etc.
- PHP code is easily embedded with HTML tags & scripts.
- PHP is one of the loosely typed languages, i.e. PHP will automatically converts the variable to its correct data type.

5.7. Operators in PHP

5.7.1. **Assignment operators (=):** = (equal) operator is used to assign values to variables (or) to assign one variable to another. Ex: $ avg = 31.42; $x = $y; $ sum = $x+$y;

5.7.2. **Arithmetic operators:** used to perform basic mathematical operations.

$ x	Negation
$ x + $ y	Addition
$ x - $ y	Subtraction
$ x * $ y	Multiplication
$ x / $ y	Division
$ x % $ y	Modulus
+=	Adds value & assigns to a variable.
-=	Subtracts the value to a variable.
***=**	Multiplies the value to a variable.
/=	Divides the value to a variable.
%=	Divides & assign modulus to a variable.
.=	Concatenates and assign the value to a variable. (Only for strings).

Ex: $ x = 9; $ x +=3;
$ x = "hello"; $ x. = "hi"; // hello hi.

5.7.3. **String Operators (.):** The dot (.) is a string concatenation operator is used to combine values to create a string. Build a string from other strings, variables and numbers.

Ex:
```
1) $str = "Hyderabad";
     echo 'my city is' .$str;
2) $echo 'my city is '. 'hyd';
```

5.7.4. **Comparison operators:** Used to compare one value with another and returns true or false based on status of the match.

==	Equal to
!=	Not equal to
<>	Not equal to

===	Identical to
!==	Not identical to
<	Less than operator
>	Greater than operator
<=	Less than or equal to operator
>=	Greater than or equal to operator

5.7.5. **Logical Operators:** Also called Boolean operators, evaluates the logical expression and return true or false.

<table>
<tr><td>AND</td><td>Represents Logical AND operation</td></tr>
<tr><td>OR</td><td>Represents Logical OR operation</td></tr>
<tr><td>XOR</td><td>Represents Logical XOR operation</td></tr>
<tr><td>&&</td><td>Represents Logical AND operation</td></tr>
<tr><td>||</td><td>Represents Logical OR operation</td></tr>
</table>

5.7.6. **Increment /Decrement operators:**

$ x++	Post increment operator
++ $ x	Pre increment operator
$ x --	Post decrement operator
--$ x	Pre decrement operator

Ex:
```
$ x =10;        $ y = $ x++;
echo $y;    //10
$ y = ++$ x;
echo $y;         //12
$ y = $ x--;     //12
$y = --$ x;    //10
```

5.7.7. **Operator Precedence:**

<table>
<tr><th>Associativity</th><th colspan="2">operators</th></tr>
<tr><td>Right</td><td>!</td><td>Logical</td></tr>
<tr><td>Left</td><td>*, /, %</td><td>Arithmetic</td></tr>
<tr><td>Left</td><td>+, -, .</td><td>Arithmetic & string</td></tr>
<tr><td>Left</td><td>&</td><td>Bitwise, references</td></tr>
<tr><td>Left</td><td>|</td><td>Bitwise</td></tr>
</table>

Left	&&	Logical
Left	||	Logical
Right	=+,=- ,=*,=/,=./=&,=| ,=^,=<<,=>>	Assignment
Left	And	Logical
Left	XOR	Logical
Left	Or	Logical
Left	,	Logical

5.7.8. **Bitwise operators** : Performs operations at bit level.

&	Bitwise AND
|	Bitwise OR
^	Bitwise XOR
!	Bitwise Not

5.8. Type Casting:

- PHP allows to convert datatype of a variable to another data type, is called "type casting".

  Ex:
```
1) $x = 35.42; $y = 20;
    $x = $x + $y;    //float
 2) $x = "4";      //string
 $x = x+3;      // 7, integer
 $x = $x+3.5;    //10.5, float or double
```

5.8.1. Explicit type Conversion:

- **var = (target-type) variable**

  $x = (Boolean) $x // converts to Boolean
  $x = (float) $x //converts to float
  Ex: $x = 34.5;
  $y = 20;
  $z = $x+$y; //float -- 54.5;
  $z = (int) $x+$y; //int – 54;
- **settype (var_name, "target type");**

  $z = $x + $y // float

settype ($z, "int"); //int

echo "$z"; //54.

Ex: settype ($x, "array"); // to array

Settype ($y, "bool"); // to Boolean

5.9. Control Structures:

5.9.1. Conditional statements:

- if statement
- if-else statement
- if-elseif – else statement
- switch-case statement → allows case constant as string also, including integer constant / char const.

5.9.2. Looping (or) Iterative statements:

- while loop
- do-while loop
- for-loop
- for each loop

- ```
  do {
   statements
  } while (condition);
  ```

- ```
  for ( initialization; condition; inc/dec)
  {
      Statements
  }
  ```
- ```
  for each (array as value)
  {
  statements
  }
  ```
- ```
  for each (array as key =>)
  {
  ```

```
Statement;
}
```

5.9.3. Jump statements

- break
- continue
- exit -- used when we want to stop a program from running. It can block infinite looping statements in the program.

Ex:
```
for($k=0;  $k<5;$k++)
    {
      If($k==3)
         {
               exit;
         }
      echo " the no is ".$i;
      echo "<br>;
    }
    echo " this is exit";
```

5.10. Arrays:

- An array is a homogeneous collection. Array elements are accessed by name and index.

  Ex: $cities = array ('hyd', 'KMNR','VJW');

  echo "the second name is $cities [1]";
- PHP supports 3 types of arrays

5.10.1. Numeric array (indexed array)

- Defines an array with a numeric ID key (index). The index value starts from '0'. The array can store number, string, object etc. the integer values as their index.

  Ex:
```
<?php
   $cities =array ("hyd", "Chennai","delhi","bopal");
   print_r($cities);
   ?> ex: $cities [2]
```

  print_r () – It is a built in function in PHP, used to print or display information stored in a variable.

print_r ($variable)

print_r ($variable, $flag)

if flag is true, the result is stored into a variable, rather than printing. By default flag is false, flag is optional.

Ex: $cities = array("hyd", "ooty", "delhi");

print_r($cities);

$res = print_r($cities, true);

echo "$res";

5.10.2. Associative Arrays

- In associative arrays, an index is associated with a value.
  Ex: employee name – key
  Salary – value.
- The values are accessed by specifying key.
  Ex: $sal = array("Teja" => 35000, "ravi"=>60000,"sahithi"=>45000);
  (OR)
  $sal ["Teja"] => 35000;
  $sal ["ravi"] => 60000;
  $sal ["sahithi"] => 45000;

5.10.3. Multidimensional Arrays

- A multidimensional array is an array of arrays. I.e. A array can contain sub array, it further has sub array and so on.

Ex:
```
$emps = array(array ("ram" =>87000, "suresh"=>
97000, "ganesh"=>99000), array("rajesh"=> 165000,
yakub"=>11500),
array("raman"=>45000,"harish"=>35000));
print_r($emps);
```

5.11. User-defined Functions in PHP

- PHP allows to write our own (user defined) functions for reusability.
- Functions make it easy to use the same piece of code several times in application.
- A function in PHP defined as

Function *<fun_name> (arg1, arg2,... argn)*

{

```
//code to execute
return expn;
}
```

- A function is declared using 'function' keyword.

5.11.1. Naming Conventions for functions

- Function names are not case sensitive. i.e., swap (), Swap (), SWAP () refers same.
- Function name has only chars, digits & under source
- Function name cannot start with digit
- Two functions can't have same name. because PHP doesn't support function overloading
- Reserved keywords cannot be used as names.

5.11.2. Scope of Variables:-

- The variables used with in a function are called local variables, the scope or visibility is local to the function. These cannot be viewed or modified outside a function.
- The variables that are declared outside the functions are global variable. Any function can view or modify.
- A function can modify a global variable by using the keyword "global".

  Ex: $x = 10;

```
function fun1 ()
  {
  global $x = 15; //global variable
}
```

5.11.3. Arguments passing methods

- Pass by value **eg**: swap ($a, $b).
- Passing arguments by reference **eg**: swap(&$a, &b)

5.11.4. Recursive Functions

- A recursive function is one that continually invokes itself under a specific condition.
- A complex problem is divided into small parts.
- Increases the flexibility & adaptability of a function.
- During recursion

  1. Must have an exit condition.
  2. Each recursive call must be different than the one before it.

```
function fact ($no)
        {
    if ($no<2)
            return 1;
    else
            return($no *fact($no-1));
  }
```

5.11.5. Variable Functions

- PHP supports variable functions.
- If a variable name has parentheses appended to it, PHP searches for a function with the same name as variable name and executes it.
- Variable functions are used to implement call backs.

5.11.6. Default parameters/ optional parameters

- It is possible to specify default parameters when building functions in PHP so that, even if a parameter is not passed to the function, it is still accessible inside the function and has a predefined value. Because they don't need to be supplied to the method, these default values can alternatively be referred to as optional parameters.
- A recursive function is one that continually invokes itself under a certain circumstance.
- Creating a default parameter in a function is very simple and is like normal variable assignment.
- A function can have any number of default parameters, as its need.
- An array can also be used as default to the end of the required parameters to avoid conflict.
- Default parameters simplify the programming necessities.

Ex:

```
<? php
   function find ($m, $n, $c=10, $d=5)
      {
            Return ($m+$n+$c+$d);
      }
   $x = find (10, 20); // 10+20+10+5
   $y = find (10, 20, 30); // 10+20+30+5
   $z = find (10, 20, 30, 40); // 10+20+30+40.
?>
```

5.12. Working with forms

- The <form> tag in HTML is used to create a HTML form for user input.
- A form can contain elements like buttons, text fields; drop down list (select), checkbox, radio buttons etc.
- The <input> element is used to add user controls to the form.

  Ex:

```
<form name = "f1">
 CSE <input type = "checkbox" name = "c1" value= "cse">
</form>
```

5.12.1. Processing a web form

- The information entered in a web form is forwarded for processing to a web server.
- The processing of web form include
  - I. Data entry on the form
  - II. Retrieving the form data
  - III. Validating the form data.

5.12.2. Submitting form data:

- There are two ways to send the form data to the server for processing.

  A. Using the get () method:-

  When 'submit' button is pressed on web form,

  - get () method sends the form data to the server by attaching it at the end of URL. (In Address bar).
  - The attached form data is called query-string.

- The get () method allows to send only a limited amount of information at a time.
- The information sent by using the get () method is displayed in the address bar of the web browser.
- Hence this approach is not used for sending passwords or any sensitive information.

B. Using the post () method:-

When 'submit' button is pressed on the form,

- Post () method appends all the data inform into HTTP header message body.
- Used to send any amount of data, i.e. used to submit large and complex web forms.
- Information sent through this method is not displayed in the URL of web browser.

5.12.3. Retrieving the form Data

A. $_GET[ ] function:-

- The built-in function $_GET [] can be used to retrieve values from a form that was received using the get () method.
- It is only for retrieving data sent through form's get method.

B. $_POST [ ] function:-

- The built-in function $_POST [] is used to get values from a form supplied using the post () method.

```
Ex:  1) <? php echo $_GET ["name"]; ? >
          2) <? php echo $_POST ["name"]; ?>
```

C. $_REQUEST [ ] function:-

- Applied to the gathering of form data transmitted via the get () and post () methods.

```
Ex: <? php echo $_REQUEST ["name"];  ? >
```

D. $ SERVER ['REQUEST_METHOD']:-

- Which methods (get or post) used by the form to send data to the server is know from this SERVER method.

```
Ex:  <? php
       if ($SERVER ['REQUEST_METHOD'] == 'get')
```

```
                echo "get method";
        else
                echo"post method";
        ?>
```

5.12.4. Validating a form

- Form validation involves, verifying that the users have entered the correct data in relevant form elements.
- The validating form on server side is more secure.

  Ex: checking for username should not be empty

```
if (! $_POST ['uname'])
     echo "enter valid user name"
else
     echo" credentials are correct."
```

5.13. Working with Databases:-

- My sql is a RDMS used by the world's largest and fastest growing organizations.
- MySQL became a part of Oracle following its acquisition of Sun in 2010.
- PHP is used to construct dynamic web pages, which need a database to store and retrieve data.
- One of the biggest contributors to open source software in the world.
- MySQL is the most used database for PHP.
- The configuration of the MySQL database server must be verified by

```
<? Php
        phpinfo ();
?>
```

5.13.1. Connecting to Database

- In PHP, a database can be utilised when connecting to the MySQL database server.
- The information required to connect to database
  - ➢ Hostname (localhost / ipaddress)
  - ➢ Database username (usually –root)
  - ➢ Password (usually "" – empty)
  - ➢ Database name (optional).
- "if connection is required in multiple pages, the 'connect' code is stored in a fix and imported like a normal file. i.e.

<? php → ***connection code***

include 'filename'; ***//calls the file.***

?>

5.13.2. Connecting to MySQL server

- The functions for connecting to server are
  mysql_connect ("hostname", "username", "password")
  (Or)
  mysql_connect ("host", "username", "password", "database name")
- **Host–** optional specifies the host name or IP address. (For local server, it is "localhost").
- **Username –** optional, it specifies mysql username.
- **Password–** optional, it specifies mysql password.
- **Database name –** optional, it is database name where operation performed on data.
- The function returns an object which represents MySQL connection. If connection failed it returns false.

```
<? php
     $con = mysqli_connect ('localhost', 'root', ' ',
     'shipment');
     if (!$con)
          die ('Error in connection',mysqli_error());
     else
          echo"Connection to server is successful";
?>
```

5.13.3. Creating database using PHP script

- The functions for creating a database is
  mysql_query(' query for create', connection)
  (Or)
  mysqli_query(connection, query).
- mysqli_query () function returns the result from database if it is successful. If the function fails return false.
- The mysqli_query () function is used to execute a query from PHP script.

5.13.4. Selecting the Database

- The functions **mysql_select_db (), mysqli_select_db ()** used to select the required database.
  mysqli_select_db (dbname, conn)

mysqli_select_db (conn, dbname).

- Return true if the selection is successful else returns false.

5.13.5. Creating a table in Database:

```
$qry1 = "CREATE TABLE login (uname varchar (60) NOT
NULL, pword varchar (10) NOT NULL)";
$ tab = mysqli_query($con, $qry1);
      if($tab)
      echo "<br> table created";
else
      echo "<br> table not created";
```

5.13.6. Inserting Data into table:

```
$ qry2 = "INSERT INTO login (uname, pword) VALUES
($name, $pwd)";
  Ex:  mysqli_query ($con, $qry2)
```

5.13.7. Retrieving Data from a table:

```
$ res = mysqli_query ($ con, "select *from login");
echo "<table border=2>";
echo "<tr> <th> user name </th>
      <th> password </th> </tr>";
while ($row = mysqli_fetch_array($res))
      {
      echo "<tr> <td>";
      echo "$row ['uname'];
      echo "</td>";
      echo"<td>";
      echo $row [ 'pword'];
      echo "</td> </tr>";
      }
echo "</table>;
```

5.13.8. Updating a record in a table:

```
$oldvalue = $_ POST ['old'];
$newvalue= $_POST ['new'];
mysqli_query ($con, "UPDATE login1 SET pword = '$new
value' WHERE pword = '$old value'");
```

5.13.9. Deleting a record from a Table:

```
$name = $_POST ['user']; -→reading from data
mysqli_query ($con, "DELETE FROM login1 WHERE uname =
'$name'");
```

5.14. Features of phpMyAdmin

- The following list of functionality that phpMyAdmin supports:
  - Databases, views, tables, columns, and indexes can all be created, modified, browsed, and deleted using phpMyAdmin.
  - It can use queries and stored procedures to display several result sets.
  - phpMyAdmin displays numerous results sets using stored procedures and queries.
  - InnoDB tables and foreign keys are supported.
  - The modifications made to databases, views, and tables can be monitored using phpMyAdmin.
  - The PDF visuals of our database layout are now available.
  - phpMyAdmin exports to a number of file types, including XML, CSV, PDF, ISO/IEC 26300 - OpenDocument Text, and Spreadsheet.
  - Mysqli, the upgraded MySQL extension, is supported.
  - phpMyAdmin supports 80 different languages for communication.
  - phpMyAdmin has the ability to edit, run, bookmark, and even run batch queries.
- It has the ability to convert saved data into any format by employing a set of pre-defined functions. BLOB-data as an image or download link, for instance.
- It offers the option to backup the database in various formats..

5.14.1. Advantage of phpMyAdmin

- Since phpMyAdmin has a web browser, it can run on any server or OS.

- The graphical interface of phpMyAdmin makes it more simpler to create, delete, and edit databases as well as manage all of its components than using the command-line editor for MySQL.
- phpMyAdmin enables us to manage user permissions and manage several servers at once.
- In addition, we can export our database's data in a variety of forms, including XML, CSV, SQL, PDF, OpenDocument Text, Excel, Word, and Spreadsheet.
- Using phpMyAdmin's graphical user interface, we can create and edit functions, triggers, and events as well as execute sophisticated SQL statements and queries.

5.14.2. Disadvantage of phpMyAdmin

- phpMyAdmin has a straightforward interface, but it might be difficult for beginners to understand.
- Installing phpMyAdmin is challenging because it requires the Apache server, PHP, and MySQL software packages.
- Unlike XAMPP, which already comes with all of these software tools in one package, we must install each of them separately. The simplest way to get phpMyAdmin is through XAMPP.
- It lacks a visualisation of the schema.
- Because phpMyAdmin is a browser-only web application, browsers are essential to its operation.
- It is not capable of auto-compilation.

5.14.3. Data Backup problem with phpMyAdmin

- Many functions are missing from phpMyAdmin's import/export functionality. The following list of phpMyAdmin backup issues is provided for your reference:
- **Scheduling** - There is no automatic mechanism to export database data in phpMyAdmin.
- **Storage media support** - Since phpMyAdmin is web-based software, which we have already covered, it can only be used via a browser. We can only create backups of our system's local discs.
- **Compression, Encryption, and other option** - The files that phpMyAdmin exports are saved as standard text files without any further processing. While keeping these files in their original form typically requires a large amount of disc space.

Open the phpMyAdmin interface by starting the Apache server and going to localhost/phpmyadmin in a web browser.

Since we set up a MySQL database during the Environment Setup, we have a root user with the password root@123. You must provide the same credentials once phpMyAdmin has opened in order to access the database.

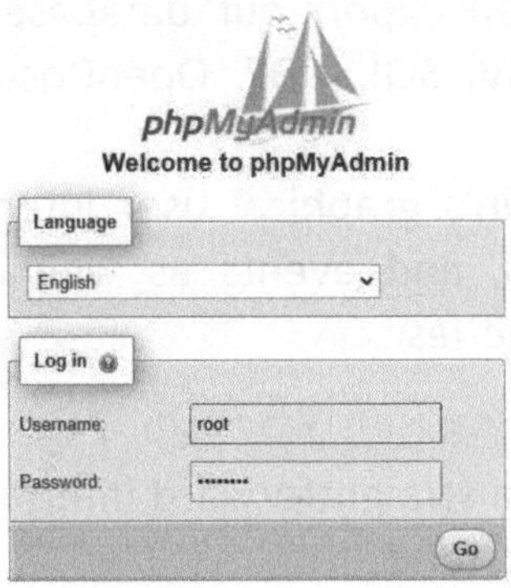

5.14.4. Dashboard

The following sections are loaded on the phpMyAdmin screen once you have logged in. The left-hand section displays the databases that are accessible, including both system- and user-created databases.

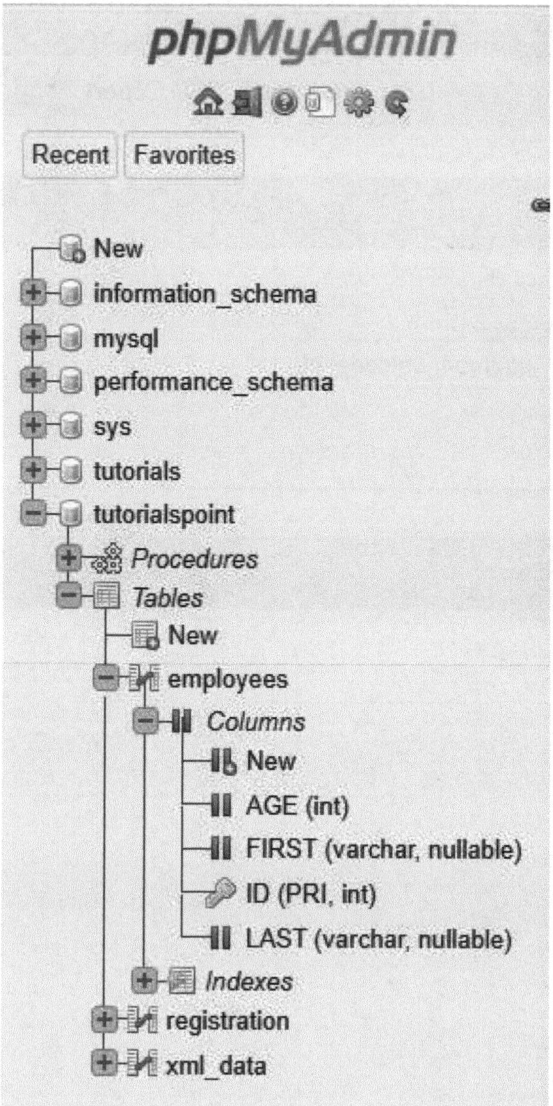

The dashboard's right side displays a tabbed interface for doing all database management tasks, as seen below.

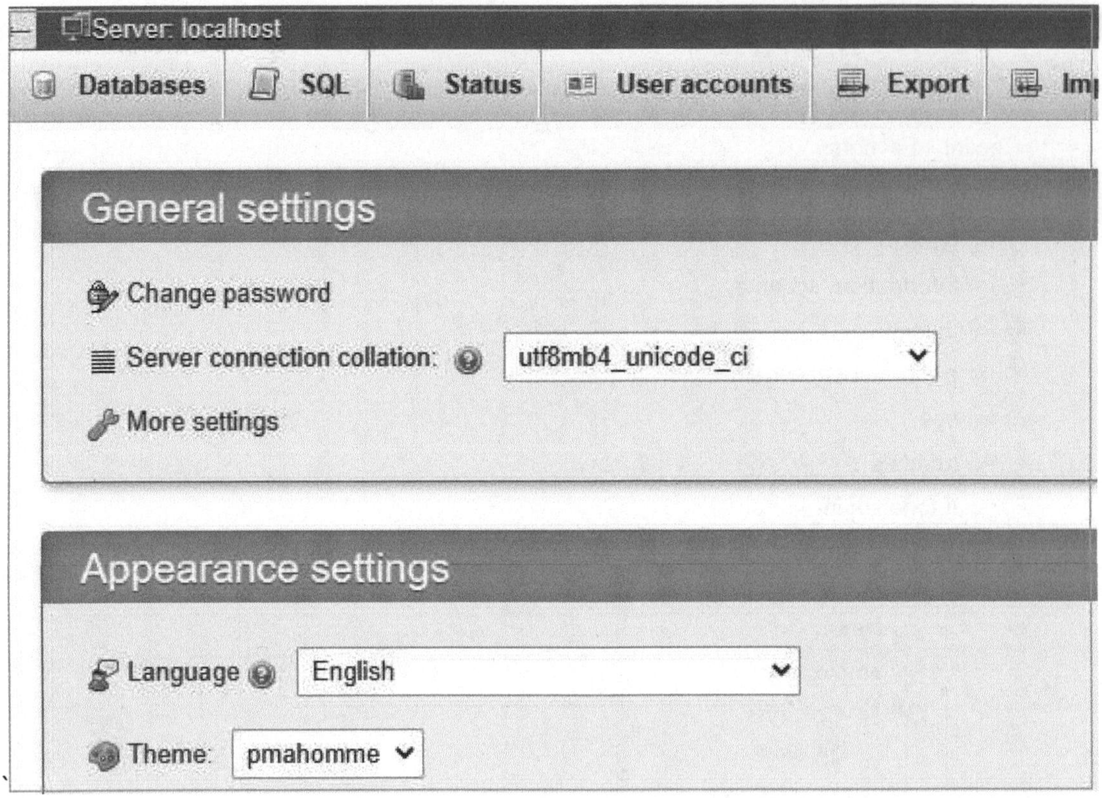
Server: localhost
Databases
SQL
Status
User accounts
Export
General settings
Change password
Server connection collation:
utf8mb4_unicode_ci
More settings
Appearance settings
Language
English
Theme:
pmahomme

5.14.5. Databases

To view a list of databases with additional information, select the Database tab. Here, we may perform various activities including database creation and database iteration.

To view a list of tables with additional information, click on any mentioned database. According to the context, tabs alter. Now, tabs will display according to the database.

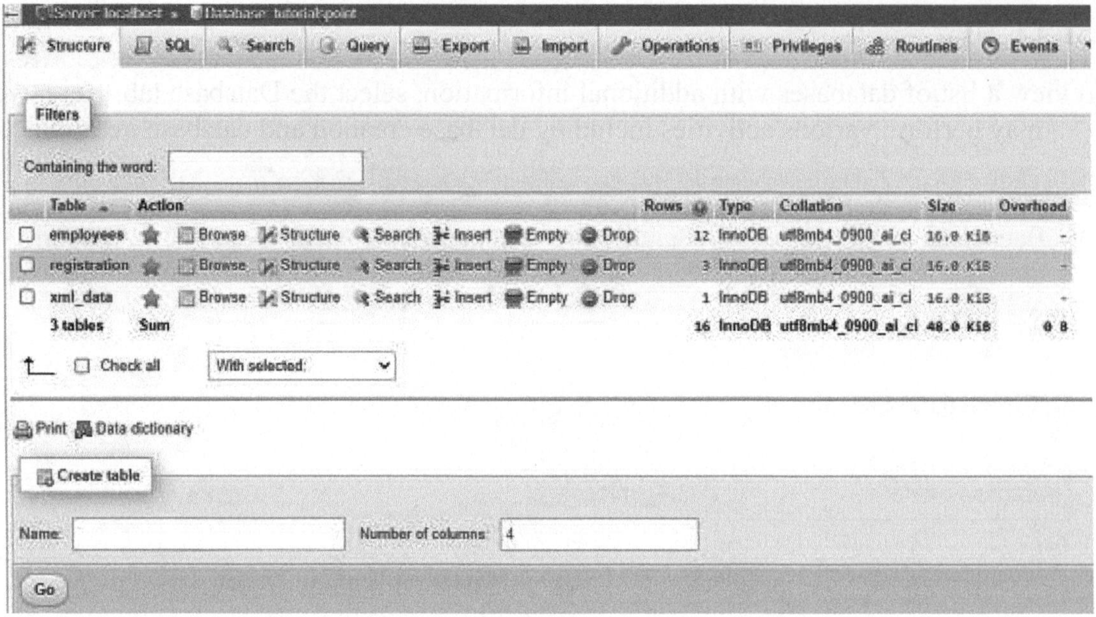
Server: localhost » Database: tutorialspoint
Structure
SQL
Search
Query
Export
Import
Operations
Privileges
Routines
Events
Filters
Containing the word:
Table
Action
Rows
Type
Collation
Size
Overhead
employees
Browse
Structure
Search
Insert
Empty
Drop
12
InnoDB
utf8mb4_0900_ai_ci
16.0 KiB
registration
3
xml_data
1
3 tables
Sum
16
48.0 KiB
0 B
Check all
With selected:
Print
Data dictionary
Create table
Name:
Number of columns:
4
Go

5.14.6. Tables

Click on any table in the schema browser right now to bring up its details and use the redesigned tabbed interface to perform the procedures outlined below on that table. –

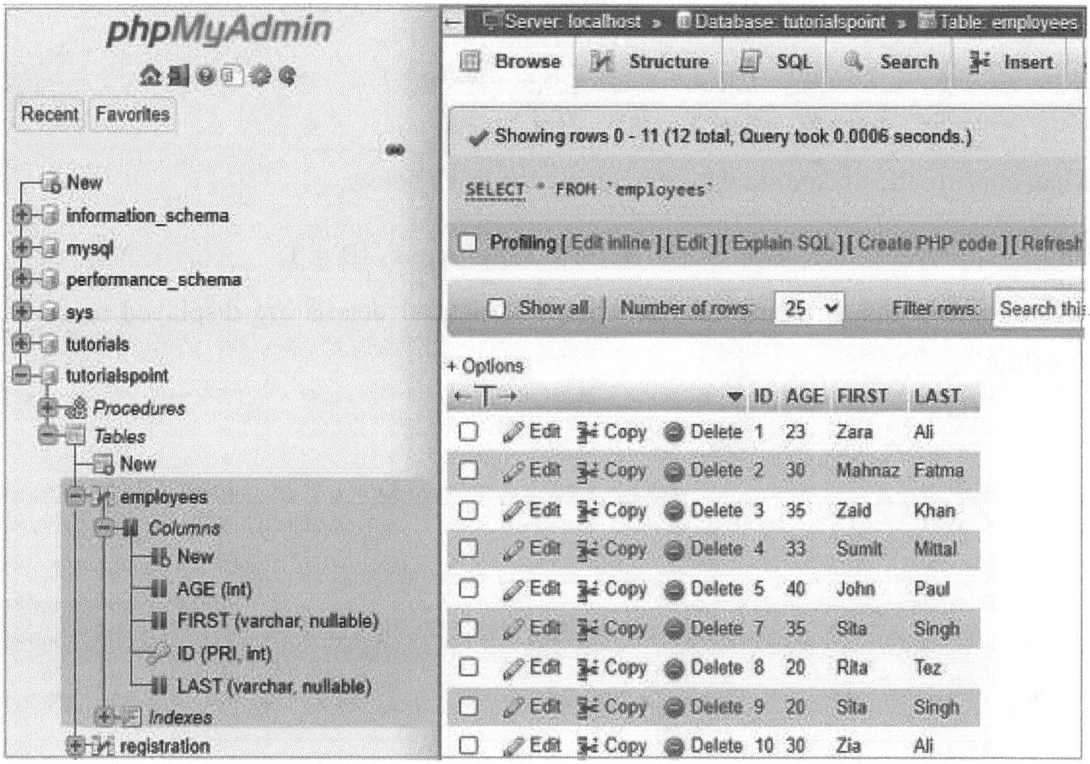

Any cell that has been double clicked becomes editable, allowing you to change and save data. The esc key has no effect on data saving. The update query and operation status will be displayed as soon as you exit the editing cell, as seen below.–

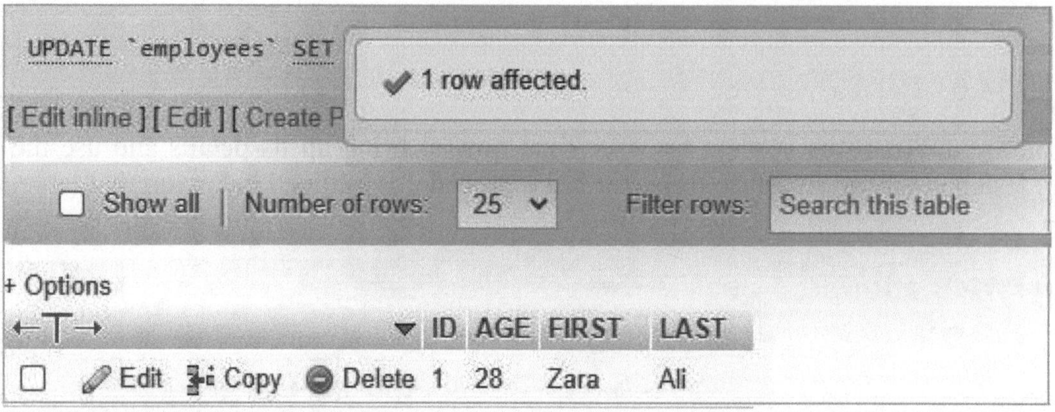

You can confirm the update statement by using the links below.

UPDATE `employees` SET `AGE` = '28' WHERE `employees`.`ID` = 1;

When you select the Structure tab, the table's structural details are displayed as seen below.

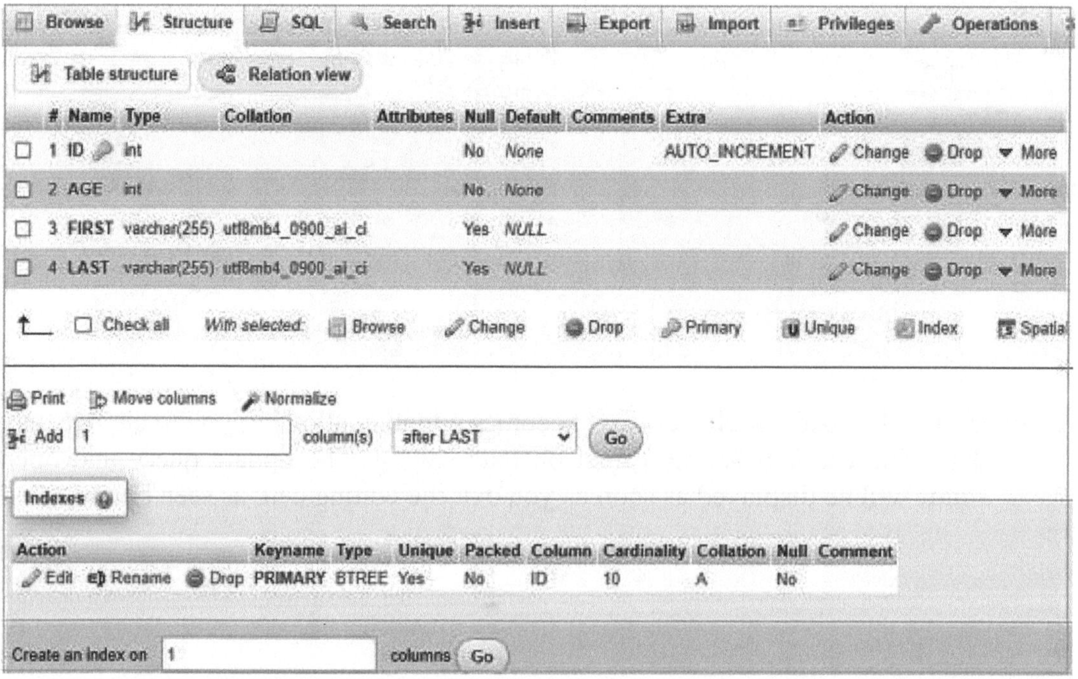

5.14.7. Bugs-Debugging

Rarely do programmes function properly on the first try. Numerous issues in your software could result in the PHP interpreter producing an error message. The location of the error messages is up to you. Messages may be transmitted to the web browser together with other application output. They may be recorded in the web server error log as well.

The display errors configuration directive must be set to On in order for error messages to appear in the browser. Set log errors to On to send errors to the web server's error log. If you want error warnings in both places, you can turn them both on.

When setting the value of error reporting in PHP, you can utilise some defined constants to ensure that only specific kinds of errors are reported: E_ PARSE (parse errors), E_ ERROR (fatal errors), E_ WARNING (warnings), E _NOTICE (notices), and E _STRICT are the error codes that can be used (strict notices).

Use PHP-aware editors for creating your PHP application, such as BBEdit or Emacs. Syntax highlighting is one of these editors' unique characteristics. Depending on what those components are, it alters the colour of those areas in your programme. Strings are pink, whereas words like "if" and "while" are blue, "comments" are grey, and "variables" are black, as examples.

Another feature that ensures the balance of your quotations and brackets is quote and bracket matching. The editor highlights the opening delimiter that it matches when you input a closing delimiter like.

The following points need to be verified while debugging the program.

- **Missing Semicolons** – A semicolon is used to end each PHP statement (;). A semicolon is the point at which PHP halts its reading of a statement. PHP continues reading the statement on the following line if you don't use a semicolon at the end of a line.
- **Not Enough Equal Signs** – Two equal signs (==) are required when determining whether two values are equal in a comparison statement. One common error is to only use one equal sign.
- **Misspelled Variable Names** – PHP interprets a misspelt variable as a brand-new variable. Keep in mind that $test and $Test are not the same variables in PHP..
- **Missing Dollar Signs** – Although it can be quite difficult to spot, a missing dollar sign in a variable name normally results in an error message that lets you know where the issue is.
- **Troubling Quotes** – It's possible to use too many, too few, or the incorrect kinds of quotations. So make sure there are a fair quantity of quotes.
- **Missing Parentheses and curly brackets** – They should always be in pairs.
- **Array Index** – All the arrays should start from zero instead of 1.

Additionally, handle all problems appropriately and direct all trace messages to the system log file so that, in the event that a problem arises, it will be recorded there and you can troubleshoot it from there.

Unit Summary

Through this unit we have understood Server-side scripting, Advance PHP Databases and Inserting data by Connecting to Server. We have also learnt Listing, Altering and Deleting Databases and Tables. In addition we have also delved into PHP myadmin and database bugs.

EXERCISE

Multiple Choice Questions

1.1 PHP stands for -

a) Hypertext Preprocessor

b) Pretext Hypertext Preprocessor

c) Personal Home Processor

d) None of the above

1.2 Variable name in PHP starts with -

a) ! (Exclamation)

b) $ (Dollar)

c) & (Ampersand)

d) # (Hash)

1.3 Which of the following function displays the information about PHP and its configuration?

a) php_info()

b) phpinfo()

c) info()

d) None of the above

1.4. Which of the following is the correct syntax to write a PHP code?

a) <?php ?>

b) < php >

c) < ? php ?>

d) <? ?>

1.5 How to define a function in PHP?

a) functionName(parameters) {function body}

b) function {function body}

c) function functionName(parameters) {function body}

d) data type functionName(parameters) {function body}

1.6 What does PDO stand for?

a) PHP Database Orientation

b) PHP Data Orientation

c) PHP Data Object

d) PHP Database Object.

1.7 Which one of the following databases has PHP supported almost since the beginning?

a) Oracle Database

b) SQL

c) SQL+

d) MySQL

1.8 The updated MySQL extension released with PHP 5 is typically referred to as ______________

a) MySQL

b) mysql

c) mysqli

d) mysqly

1.9 Which one of the following statements is used to create a table?

a) CREATE TABLE table_name (column_name column_type);

b) CREATE table_name (column_type column_name);

c) CREATE table_name (column_name column_type);

d) CREATE TABLE table_name (column_type column_name);

1.10 Which method returns the error code generated from the execution of the last MySQL function?

a) errno() b) errnumber()

c) errorno() d) errornumber()

Answers of Multiple Choice Questions

1.5 (a) 1.2 (b) 1.3 (b) 1.4 (d) 1.5 (c)1.6 (c) 1.7(d) 1.8 (c) 1.9 (a)1.10(a)

Short and Long Answer Type Questions

Category I

1.1 Compare and contrast the client and server-side scripting?
1.2 Write the characteristics of PHP?
1.3 List the features of PHP?

Category II

1.4 Discus about PHP MyAdmin?
1.5 Write a program to connect to database using PHP?
1.6 List the records in data base using PHP MyAdmin?

References and suggested readings

1. The Joy of PHP Programming: A Beginner's Guide to Programming Interactive Web Applications with PHP and MySQL Author – Alan Forbes
2. PHP & MySQL Novice to Ninja Author – Tom Butler & Kevin Yank Latest Edition – Sixth Edition
3. Head First PHP & MySQL Author – Lynn Beighley & Michael Morrison Latest Edition – First Edition Publisher – O'Reilly
4. P HP: A Beginner's Guide Author – Vikram Vaswani Latest Edition – First Edition Publisher – McGraw-Hill Education
5. PHP In Action: Objects, Design, Agility Author – Daginn Reiersol, Chris Shiflett, and Marcus Baker Latest Edition – 1st Edition Publisher – Manning Publications

Dynamic QR CODE for further reading

References for further learning

The best way to learn Web technologies is by trying out programmes yourself. Following are certain references which I have found useful. There must be other numerous resources as well.

[1] HTML and CSS: Design and Build Websites by Jon Duckett

[2] Learning Web Design: A Beginner's Guide to HTML, CSS, JavaScript, and Web Graphics by Jennifer Niederst Robbins

[3] Web Development and Design Foundations with HTML5 by Terry Felke-Morris

[4] JavaScript and jQuery: Interactive Front-End Web Development by Jon Duckett

[5] HTML5 and CSS3: Responsive Web Design Cookbook by Benjamin LaGrone

[6] Responsive Web Design with HTML5 and CSS: Develop future-proof responsive websites using the latest HTML5 and CSS by Ben Frain

[7] Mastering Web Application Development with AngularJS by Pawel Kozlowski

[8] Node.js Web Development, 4th Edition by David Herron and Brad Dayley

[9] Flask Web Development: Developing Web Applications with Python by Miguel Grinberg

[10] The Complete Guide to Web Development for Beginners by Arianne Dee

CO AND PO ATTAINMENT TABLE

Course outcomes (COs) for this course can be mapped with the programme outcomes (POs) after the completion of the course and a correlation can be made for the attainment of POs to analyze the gap. After proper analysis of the gap in the attainment of POs necessary measures can be taken to overcome the gaps.

Table for CO and PO attainment

Course Outcomes	Attainment of Programme Outcomes (1- Weak Correlation; 2- Medium correlation; 3- Strong Correlation)						
	PO-1	**PO-2**	**PO-3**	**PO-4**	**PO-5**	**PO-6**	**PO-7**
CO-1	3	3	3	2	1	1	2
CO-2	3	3	3	2	1	1	2
CO-3	3	3	3	2	1	1	2
CO-4	3	3	3	2	1	1	2
CO-5	3	3	3	2	1	1	2
CO-6	3	3	3	2	1	1	2

The data filled in the above table can be used for gap analysis.

INDEX